ALL THE MONEY IN THE WORLD

BKF9805431

ALL THE MONEY IN THE WORLD

THE ART AND HISTORY OF PAPER MONEY AND COINS FROM ANTIQUITY TO THE 21ST CENTURY

DOUGLAS MUDD

CURATOR, AMERICAN NUMISMATIC ASSOCIATION MONEY MUSEUM

Collins

An Imprint of HarperCollinsPublishers

First Edition

Produced by: Facts That Matter, Inc.
Book Concept by: Les Krantz
Designed by: Jensie Lauritsen, Nei-Turner Media Group

The name of the "Smithsonian," "Smithsonian Institution," and the sunburst logo are registered trademarks of the Smithsonian Institution.

Library of Congress Cataloging-in-Publication Data
ISBN-10: 0-0-6088837-7
ISBN13: 978-0-06-088837-4

06 07 08 09 10   10 9 8 7 5 4 3 2 1

In Memory of Mrs. Elvira Eliza Clain-Stefanelli,
who started me down this path.

Acknowledgements

This project began six years ago, when I received a phone call at my work in the Smithsonian Institution's National Numismatic Collection from someone I had never met before who had just published a book entitled *The Art of the Market*. The person turned out to be the co-author and publisher, Les Krantz, who wanted to create a follow-up book on the art of money, using the same high standards of writing and imagery. After several phone conversations and a visit to the National Numismatic Collection, the idea began to take shape, and I began to photograph and write what would become the core chapters of this book. Then in 2005, Les and I reconnected and began to work on the book in earnest, with the result you see today. I would like to thank Les for persevering in this drawn-out project and believing in my ability to get it done.

Many people have contributed to this project, not least those who have influenced my growth as a numismatist, especially Elvira Eliza Clain-Stefanelli, Dr. Richard (Dick) G. Doty, Robert Hoge, and my father, among others. All have profoundly influenced my thinking and approach to the science of numismatics. I would especially like to thank Dick for reading over the manuscript for this book and his comments. Jim Hughes was instrumental in helping gather information on the coins and paper money from the National Numismatic Collection, as were Ross Watson and Guido Fenzi—without their help this work would have been much more difficult to complete. I would also like to thank Charles L. Mitton for generously loaning objects from his collection for use in the book. Thanks also go to Tim Knight for his editing.

My final thanks go out to my family, whose support made this book possible—especially my wife, Patti, for reading over and commenting on the manuscript, and to her and our daughter, Loren, for their patience while I spent long evenings writing the manuscript and editing images.

Douglas Mudd
Colorado Springs, Colorado
February 10, 2006

Dr. Richard G. Doty has been the Curator of Numismatics at the Smithsonian Institution's National Museum of American History since 1986. He earned his BA in 1964 and PhD in 1968, and was a college professor for six years. His work has gone in two directions: 1) to get into the mechanics/technology behind monetary production; and 2) to make modern numismatics as legitimate a branch of learning as ancient numismatics. Dr. Doty is the recipient of the Millennium Medal of the Royal Numismatic Society for his work in numismatics and has written nine books, about two hundred articles, and numerous radio scripts for the ANA and NPR.

FOREWORD

It was my pleasure to work with Douglas Mudd at the Smithsonian Institution for a dozen years. During that time, I came to know him as an accomplished general numismatist, with a particular passion for ancient Greek coinage, but also a cheerful ability to tackle any numismatic question that came his way. I also found that he was an accomplished educator, able to attract people of all ages, including children, to the pleasures of what, in less-skilled hands, has often been regarded as dull and dry, not worth a second glance. It takes a distinct set of gifts to bring the sheen, the allure, to numismatics that it ought to have. Douglas Mudd has these gifts. I often said to myself, "I wish he'd set all of this down in the form of a book, so that he could reach a wider audience." And now he has.

All the Money in the World is a very special book. Aimed at the beginning collector, it can nonetheless be read— and read with profit—by specialists as well. His writing on the origins of money (and his astute observations on what money is, and is not) puts the book on a very firm foundation from the very beginning. And his subsequent chapters, whether concentrating on money of the Americas, the Far East, the ancient world, or any of the other regions of the globe, assure us that we are in very capable hands. I was most impressed with Mudd's observations about the interconnectedness of all of the various branches of numismatics; his realization that nothing sits on the sidelines, unrelated to anything else; and his awareness that minor causes can sometimes have the most amazing and distant effects. This depth of understanding is the mark of a genuine historian, and we see it all too infrequently in numismatics—or in other branches of historical investigation.

The author does not confine himself to coinage. There is a very valuable, wide–ranging discussion of today's most common, "official" type of money—paper currency—detailing its origins and spread, its possibilities, and problems. The stories of coins and currency alike are attractively illustrated, so the book is a delight both to see and to read.

I hope you enjoy *All the Money in the World* as much as I did. I think you will.

Richard G. Doty
Senior Curator, National Numismatic Collection
Smithsonian Institution

CONTENTS

THE HISTORY OF MONEY

oinage has attracted a major part of mankind's attention since its invention in Asia Minor in the seventh century BC. It has had many uses over the ages beyond its original development for purposes of long-distance trade and military power. Among the most important and least studied is the use of money as a means of communication through art. A nation's money is often the first impression a visitor gets of the nature of a country. As such, the designs and legends placed on money have always been considered important by the authorities responsible for their issue. These authorities have often risen beyond the demands of simple utility and required that their currency be beautiful as well as useful. The focus of this book is on the art of paper money as it appears today in circulating currency, but in order to make sense of why paper money looks the way it does, it is necessary to look at the origins and history of money.

Approaching such a vast topic can be daunting—this book is a general survey of the subject emphasizing the beauty and variety of art as it has appeared on money, with an emphasis on more recent developments in paper money over the last 200 years. I will start

DETAIL OF: Australia, Ten Dollars, Bicentennial of British Settlement, 1988
Australia was the first country in the world to have a complete system of banknotes based on plastic (polymer) technology. These notes provide much greater security against counterfeiting and last four times longer than conventional paper notes. This polymer was first used on a commemorative $10 note in 1988, which marked the bicentennial of European settlement in Australia. The back depicts the ship HMS Supply from the First Fleet, with Sydney Cove in the background, as well as a group of people illustrating the diversity of Australia's modern population.

Indian Ocean, Traditional Money, Cowrie Shells, Second Millennium BC to Twentieth Century
Cowrie shells were used as money in Africa, India, China, and many of the lands in between for millennia. This image displays an array of cowrie shells, including a string of small cowries that might have been used in China during the second millennium BC. Imitations of cowries were the basis for some of China's earliest metal money.

Athens, Silver Tetradrachm, 449–413 BC
Athens became a major Greek naval power during the fifth century. After the Persian Wars, Athens was the dominant naval power of the eastern Mediterranean. It was a great commercial power as well, and created an international trade coinage with its "owls." First produced in the 490s BC, these coins were imitated for centuries in many parts of the ancient world. This coin depicts Athena, the patron goddess of Athens, and an owl, a symbol of wisdom and the avatar of Athena.

with an outline of the origins of the three major traditions of currency, which began independently in Asia Minor, India, and China over 2500 years ago. Over the last two millennia these traditions have merged into modern conceptions of how money should be used and what it should look like. The bulk of the book is divided into sections by region, with each region incorporating the recent paper money of several countries chosen for the beauty of their money and their relative importance to the history of art on money. By approaching the subject in this way, I hope to instill in the reader a sense of the regional similarities of money, and perhaps get a sense of the artistic development and diversity of modern money over time as a result of cultural exchange and technological development.

THE ORIGINS OF MONEY

Whatever medium people use for the exchange of goods or services is considered to be a form of money. Money can also be a means of storing or accumulating wealth—in some cultures "money" has a purely ceremonial or prestige purpose, in which the value of the object rests not in what it can buy, but what it represents. Many cultures have gotten along without money altogether. Other cultures have used diverse materials such as rocks, shells, feathers, and teeth. More commonly, domesticated animals and metal ingots of various shapes and sizes have been used as money. This book is concerned with money from the time that people began to embellish the design of their money; this embellishment began with the use of metallic forms of currency, especially coins. Money, in the form of replicas of tools or ingots marked with information identifying the issuing authority in order to guarantee its value (originally by weight and bullion content), or as small metal disks, was simultaneously invented in Asia within three separate cultural areas during the first millennium BC. These areas were in Asia Minor, India, and China.

THE GREEK TRADITION

The use of precious metals as money began with the ancient civilizations of the Near East. As early as 2000 BC in both Mesopotamia and Egypt, the practice emerged of carefully weighing pieces of gold and silver to determine their value in paying tribute to local rulers, placing offerings at sacred temples, and performing business transactions. The early history of money in the Mediterranean world begins with the Greek coinage tradition, invented in Asia Minor in the early seventh century BC. Small lumps of electrum (a naturally occurring alloy of silver and gold) were stamped front and back to officially identify them as being of a certain weight and fineness, thus making them more convenient in trade. In the hands of the ancient Greeks, coins soon evolved into the first "world currency" for foreign exchange. The enduring prototype for most modern coins—the flat, round, two-sided silver staters issued by the Greek city-states, and later by the extensive kingdoms established by Alexander the Great and his successors—became the standard medium for trade throughout the Mediterranean world, the Near East, and Western Europe.

In shaping our assumptions about what constitutes money and how it can be used, the Greek coinage tradition has had the greatest influence on the form and appearance of modern currency. The first coins were irregular lumps of electrum produced in a number of carefully weighed denominations with simple designs. The designs were transferred to the coins by placing the lump (or "blank") on an anvil-mounted die engraved with the desired design, and hammering a metal punch into the blank (the process of "striking" a coin). The development of this process was heavily influenced by Middle Eastern seals, which had been used for millennia to "seal" documents, to identify important individuals, and as royal symbols of approval. Making seals required carving designs in reverse into a small cylinder or a semi-precious stone, which would then be pressed into clay or wax to make an impression. The earliest coin

Macedonia, Alexander III, "the Great," Silver Tetradrachm, 336–323 BC
Alexander the Great created the world's first "world" coinage in the wake of his conquests as a means of tying his empire together (and to pay his troops). This coinage was made possible by the capture of the huge treasuries of gold and silver hoarded by the Persians for generations at their major cities, such as Ctesiphon and Babylon. Alexander's coinage was unique for the time, because it was struck at literally dozens of mints throughout his empire, all with the same designs. Coins struck in cities as far apart as Pella in Macedonia, Alexandria in Egypt, and Susa in Persia (modern Iran) could therefore be traded as a single currency throughout Alexander's realm. Tetradrachms with Alexander's designs continued to be struck for over two centuries in many cities throughout Asia Minor and beyond.

Lydia, Croesus, Gold One-Third Stater, 561–546 BC
King Croesus of Lydia is credited with creating the first bimetallic coinage in silver and gold. Previously, electrum had been used for coins, probably because electrum was found naturally in the rivers of central Asia Minor, where coinage was invented. This coin is a gold "trite" or one-third stater, with a design incorporating the foreparts of a lion and a bull facing each other. This design was a modification of the royal badge of the Lydian Mermnad dynasty, which had two lion's heads facing each other, and appeared as a lion's head on earlier electrum coins.

engravers drew on the seal engraving traditions in creating their dies and on metallurgical knowledge for the striking process. Coins are still produced using the same basic method for coin production, with the addition of modern technology and mechanical power to speed up the process.

The issuance of coinage has been a prerogative of the state almost from its invention—the kings of Lydia, including King Croesus, were the first to use their royal badges on coinage, thus guaranteeing their value. When the Greeks adopted the idea of money from the Lydians, the issuance of money became inextricably identified with political independence—coinage had become the "calling card" of independent nations. As such, the artistic quality of the coinage in the Greek tradition became increasingly important, along with the use of symbols and badges allowing for the easy identification of the issuing authority of the money. Thus the Lydians issued coins with the foreparts of a bull and a lion facing each other—the badge used on their royal seal—while Greek coins used inscriptions and symbolic images to identify their cities of origin.

The Romans elaborated on the Greek monetary tradition by further developing the art of portraiture and developing the use of messages on coins into a fine art. The foundation of the Roman Empire by Augustus formed a turning point in the use of coinage not simply as an economic tool and an international calling card, but also as an internal political tool. The imperial administration developed Roman coinage into an unrivaled media for

Syracuse, Silver Decadrachm, circa 480–460 BC
This coin, known as the "Demareteion," was one of the first decadrachm coins ever issued. All coins of this denomination were special issues designed to commemorate important events and were struck in small numbers. This coin holds a special place in numismatic history for several reasons. It was produced by one of the first master engravers of the ancient world, whose work is identifiable in other pieces from Syracuse and Leontinoi. The coin represents an early masterpiece of coin design from the transitional period of Greek art—the shift from the archaic to the classical style. And it is a coin associated with ancient literature, from whence it derives its nickname. The story goes that Queen Demarete, wife of the Syracusan tyrant Gelon, intervened to save Carthaginian prisoners captured by her husband after a great victory in 480 BC. In gratitude, the Carthaginians gave Demarete a fabulous golden crown. The proceeds from this crown were used to produce the extraordinary issue of decadrachms in celebration of Gelon's victory.

Roman Empire, Augustus, Silver Tetradrachm of Ephesus, 27 BC–14 AD
Augustus was the first Roman emperor, ruling from 27 BC to 14 AD. His reforms created a standardized imperial coinage, which featured his head on the obverse of nearly all of the coins. This feature was copied in the provincial cities for their own issues. The cistophorus was a denomination equivalent to three denarii used in the eastern branches of the empire, where it passed as a tetradrachm, the traditional large silver denomination of the Greek east.

the dissemination of official propaganda. In an age where there were no posters or newspapers, coins became a primary source of news for what was going on throughout the empire. Thus, coins were used to praise the accomplishments of the Emperors and the Roman army. Nero is celebrated for bringing peace to the Empire; Vespasian celebrates his

conquest of Judea; and the coins of Constantius II and Magnentius show the increasing Christianization of the later Roman Empire.

There are currently two major branches of the Western coinage tradition—the European and the Islamic traditions. The branching of the two

UPPER LEFT: Roman Empire, Nero, Orichalcum Sestertius, 54–68 AD
The sestertius was the Roman money of account by which wealth was calculated from the first century BC through the second century AD. Augustus reformed Roman money, as well as politics and civic culture. His monetary reform included the regular issue of bronze coinage, which had ceased during the civil wars. Among several new coin denominations was the sestertius, which was equivalent to one-fourth of a silver denarius. These coins are very popular with collectors due to their size, artistic appeal, and the variety of designs to be found on them. The image on the reverse of this coin celebrates Nero's accomplishments by showing the temple of Janus in Rome with its doors closed. This image symbolizes the peaceful state of the Roman Empire under Nero's leadership.

LOWER LEFT: Roman Empire, Vespasian, Orichalcum Sestertius , 69–79 AD
The sestertius was the largest of the bronze denominations established by Augustus at the beginning of the Roman Empire. The reverse of this coin is a common type in the Roman series—it celebrates the defeat of a Roman enemy. In this case, Vespasian is celebrating the defeat of the Judean rebels in 70 AD. This type is particularly interesting because of the details of national dress that are often included in the images of defeated enemies.

UPPER RIGHT: Roman Empire, Magnentius, Bronze Centenionalis, 350–353 AD
The name centenionalis is applied to one of a series of short-lived denominations of bronze Roman coins introduced during the mid-fourth century AD, for which we do not have the ancient names. The inscription SALUS DDNN AUG ET CAES wishes health for the reigning Augusti (Emperors) and Caesars (Vice-Emperors). By this time, Christianity was the official religion of the Roman Empire, as evidenced by the use of the Chi Rho symbol on the reverse.

LOWER RIGHT: Roman Empire, Antioch, Constantius II, Gold Solidus, 337–361 AD
Constantius II's father, Constantine I, introduced the solidus to replace the old aureus. The new coin was struck at seventy-two to the Roman pound, as opposed to the old standard of sixty to the pound. The solidus became the standard gold denomination of the Byzantine Empire and was destined to play an important role in international trade for the next 800 years.

Umayyad Caliphate, Silver Dirhem of Abd al Malik, 698–699 AD
This coin is representative of the first purely Islamic series of coins. Since many Muslims considered figural representation blasphemous, inscriptions and geometric figures became the dominant elements of Islamic coin design. Inscriptions incorporated passages from the Koran, as well as information about the year, mint location, and ruler who issued the coin. Emphasis on inscriptions as a major design element in Islamic art provided an impetus for the development of many different beautiful letterforms and scripts, some of which were specifically designed for use on coins.

Spain, Visigothic Kingdom, Gold Tremissus of Wittiza, 698–710 AD
With the fall of the western branches of the Roman Empire and the conquest of Spain, first by the Vandals and then by the Visigoths, coinage virtually ceased. The coins that were produced tended to imitate the old Roman coinage system and were based on the smaller denominations of gold (i.e., the semissus and tremissus or one-half and one-third of the solidus).

Sicily, Frederick II, Gold Augustale, 1197–1250 AD
The Holy Roman Emperor Frederick II introduced these coins in 1231 in his capacity as King of Sicily. They were issued on the same standard as the Byzantine hyperperon, which was no longer available, and set the stage for the revival of gold coinages in Western Europe. This issue was made possible by the opening of new trade routes into western North Africa, which was a major source for gold.

Venetian Republic, Nicolas Tron, Silver Lira Tron, 1472
The "Lira Tron" is the first example of a lira coin (the lira had previously been a money of account, but had never been produced as an actual coin). Nicolas Tron, Doge (Duke) of the Venetian Republic, issued this silver coin in 1472. Interestingly, the coin created a bitter controversy over the use of the Doge's portrait—portraits on coins were associated with monarchies and monarchical ambitions. (The same debate would later be waged in the United States over the design for the first U.S. coins. There was a strong movement to put George Washington's portrait on U.S. coinage, but Washington absolutely refused on the basis that portrait coins were symbols of absolute monarchies.) The design of the coin incorporates a lion, the symbol of Saint Mark, the patron saint of Venice. The lira eventually became the standard denomination of unified Italy.

Kingdom of Naples & Sicily, Emperor Charles V, Gold Ducat, 1516–1556
Emperor Charles V was born in 1500, the son of Philip of Burgundy, grandson of Maximilian I, and the grandson of Spain's King Ferdinand & Queen Isabella. These family connections meant that he inherited Burgundy and the Netherlands (1506), Spain, including the kingdom of Naples and Sicily (in 1516 as Charles I), Austria, Hungary, and the crown of the Holy Roman Empire (1519). By far the most powerful and wealthy monarch in Europe, Emperor Charles V subsequently extended his empire around the globe.

traditions occurred with the rise of Islam in the seventh century AD. By the eighth century the Umayyad dynasty of Syria had created a new coinage conforming to the principles of Islam. This coinage was characterized by the absence of figural representation and the use of calligraphy and geometric ornaments as elements of design. Beautiful scripts were created especially for use on coins and in monumental inscriptions.

Meanwhile, the European coin tradition continued to develop in the Greco-Roman style, as transmitted through the barbarian kingdoms of the West and Byzantium until the fifteenth century. The end of the 1400s witnessed the opening up of large new supplies of silver in central Europe, followed shortly afterwards by the discovery of the New World, with its vast supplies of silver and gold. The availability of silver, increased commercial activity, and the conscious classicism of the Renaissance combined to produce a new series of large-size portrait coins that became the basis for modern coinage.

THE CHINESE TRADITION

The kings of the Zhou State invented Chinese coinage in the late seventh to early sixth century BC. During the violent Warring States period, from 475 to 221 BC, China was divided into a number of culturally similar but politically divided kingdoms, all of which were issuing copper or bronze money. Each of the kingdoms had different preferred forms for their money—the forms included imitations of knives, spades, and cowrie shells (the cowrie, imported from the Indian Ocean, had long been used in the Far East as a form of money).

These objects, shaped like miniature agricultural tools, were used as coinage and had inscriptions, including a place-name, weight, or clan-name. The Qin dynasty, which unified China, produced the first round coins with a hole in the center, called ban liang, in the third century BC. These were the prototype for the famous "cash" coins that became the characteristic coin of the Far East. An interesting characteristic of Chinese coinage is that their coins were cast, not

UPPER LEFT: China, Bronze Spade Money, 300 BC
The Chinese began using objects as money at a very early date. Among these "monetized" objects were cowrie shells and tools. The tools most commonly used as money were spades and knives, both of which became increasingly stylized over time. This "coin" represents a bronze spade with characters that identify where it was made.

LOWER LEFT: China, Bronze I Pi Ch'ien (Ant Nose Money), Fourth–Third Centuries BC
This coin is an early example of manufactured coinage in China. This type of coinage was originally modeled after cowrie shells. As time went on, the "coins" became less cowrielike, as characters were placed on them that identified either the issuer or the city where the piece was created.

UPPER RIGHT: China, Wen, Bronze Ban Liang, 179–157 BC
This coin represents one of the earliest types of Chinese round coinage. Over time the design of these coins was refined and standardized. Changes included the addition of an outer rim to the coin, as well as a rim for the central square hole, and the addition of two more characters in the inscription. Chinese coins were cast in molds, unlike Western coinages, which were struck. The hole in the middle made the coins convenient to carry in strings typically of one hundred.

LOWER RIGHT: China, Ta Huang, Bronze Five Cash, 229–252 AD
This coin represents a further development of Chinese cast coinage. It now has a four-character inscription that identifies the dynastic era and the denomination of the coin, and has rims on both the outer and inner edges.

struck, and that they did not use precious metal for coins until the twentieth century. The fact that the coins were cast allowed for mass production using relatively unskilled labor in order to make up for the lack of large-denomination coins in other metals.

THE INDIAN TRADITION

India has a native coin tradition that dates back to the sixth century BC, before the conquests of Alexander the Great and his successors. The earliest coins consisted of slightly concave bars or flattened pieces of silver stamped with geometric symbols known as punch-marked coins. Struck on the Persian weight standard, these coins were produced in Northwest India and became the standard metallic currency of the eastern provinces of the Achaemenid Persian Empire and, later, the Mauryan Empire in Northern India. One of the most interesting features of early Indian coinage is the relatively loose connection it has with the rulers by and for whom they were struck—rulers were rarely named or portrayed on Indian coins.

The Indian tradition was partially submerged by Greek ideas about coinage use and design after Alexander the Great's conquests, but reappeared in bilingual coinages and in alterations in the traditional round shape of Greek coins. These Indo-Greek coins are especially important to our knowledge of this period of Indian history, the fourth century BC to the first century AD. Coins are often the only evidence we have of the existence of many kingdoms and their rulers. Over the next two millennia a vast array of types and denominations in all metals, shapes, and sizes were produced, reflecting the many influences upon the coinage of the sub-continent, including Greco-Roman, Iranian, Islamic, and finally European.

India, Mauryan Empire, Silver Karshapana, Fourth Century BC
The first Indian coins were produced in the eastern provinces of the Achaemenid Persian Empire, just before the conquests of Alexander the Great. After Alexander's departure from India, Chandragupta Maurya founded the Mauryan Empire. Mauryan money was copied from Greek models. The coins were known as "punch-marked" coins because they were struck with several small punches, rather than a single die for both sides. These punches incorporated a variety of designs, including Hindu deities and abstract symbols. Karshapanas such as this one were used for many centuries alongside Indo-Greek, Kushan, and other coinage.

Kushan Empire, Huvishka, Gold Stater, 143–180 AD
The Kushans were a branch of the nomadic Yueh-Chi tribe of central Asia. During the first century BC, they conquered a huge empire consisting of northern Afghanistan, what is now Pakistan, and large parts of northwestern India. The Bactrian Greeks, whose influence can be seen on Kushan coinage, had controlled much of this region. This region was immensely important and wealthy due to the famous Silk Road trade routes that ran from China to Europe.

HISTORY OF PAPER MONEY

Paper money has become the mainstay of modern currencies throughout the world. As an example, the total value of paper money circulating in the United States accounts for approximately nine-tenths of the circulating money in the country. Some countries have abandoned coinage altogether, due to the costs of producing coins and to economic instability. This reliance on paper money is a far cry from the situation at the beginning of the twentieth century when gold, in the form of bullion or as coinage, predominated as the basis for most of the world's money. International trade and payments were made through the transfer of gold coins and bullion whose value was based on their intrinsic gold content, not on any value set by the issuing government. Banknotes were considered, at best, a substitute for "real" money of coined gold. Most paper was directly backed by gold through a specific clause on the note itself, stating that it could be exchanged at a certain bank or treasury location for an equivalent value in gold (or sometimes silver) coins.

This situation changed during the course of the twentieth century as war, economic disaster, and the increasing volume and pace of trade forced countries to adapt their currencies. World War I shifted the financial focus of the world from war-torn and debt-ravaged Europe to the United States. The Great Depression forced most nations of the world to cease producing gold coinage in order to protect their currencies—which were still backed by gold—from collapse as gold disappeared from circulation. In 1933, the United States ceased to produce gold coins and officially demonetized gold, making it illegal for American citizens to hold gold other than as jewelry or collectible objects such as old coins.

By the start of the fourth quarter of the century, most coinage throughout the world had become fiduciary in nature—its value was determined by the issuing authority and had nothing to do with its metallic content. This was true too of the paper money, which increasingly relied on the trust of citizens in their government's stability and ability to continue to pay its debts. The typical payment clause on modern paper money is similar to that

UPPER: United States, Twenty-Dollar Gold Coin Note, Series of 1905
Detail of promise to pay

LOWER: Great Britain, Bank of England, Twenty-Pound Note, 1999
Detail of promise to pay

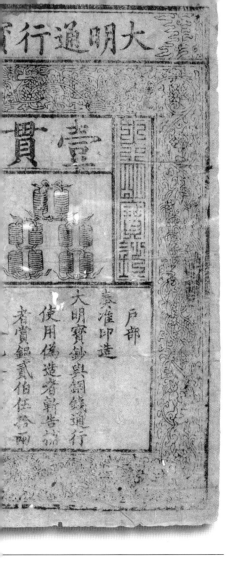

China, Ming Dynasty, One Kuan Note, Fourteenth Century
This note is an example of the earliest surviving paper money. One kuan is equivalent to 1000 copper cash coins, as is shown by the pictorial representation on the note of ten strings of one hundred cash each. These notes were issued from 1374 onward, but the Chinese had paper money from at least the eighth century AD. Marco Polo was the first Westerner to report on the use of paper money by the Chinese under the Yuan (Mongol) dynasty during the thirteenth century.

which appears on American Federal Reserve Notes: "This note is legal tender for all debts, public and private." Gone are any assurances that the bearer can exchange the note for gold, silver, or any other commodity—paper currency is accepted as money with value in and of itself, not just as a convenient substitute for value despite its negligible intrinsic worth. This represents a major historical shift in public attitudes towards money.

Historically, the use of paper money as a circulating medium was closely related to shortages of metal for coins. The earliest paper money originated in China around the seventh century AD during the Tang dynasty, in the form of privately issued bills of credit or exchange notes with a date limitation. During the tenth century, the Song dynasty, short of copper for striking coins, issued the first generally circulating notes. These notes were a promise to redeem the bearer at a later specified date for some commodity, usually specie.

Paper money, as we know it, was invented when the government of the Jin dynasty began issuing Exchange Certificates without a date limitation in 1189. The Mongol Yuan dynasty (1206–1367) used paper money exclusively, going so far as to completely ban the use of metal in the form of coins or bullion for exchange. This was the situation that Marco Polo encountered on his sojourn in China with his uncle and father from 1275 to 1292. The idea of paper substituting gold and silver was a total surprise even to the mercantile Polos. Marco attributed the success of paper money to Kublai Khan's stature as a ruler: *"With these pieces of paper they can buy anything and pay for anything. And I can tell you that the papers that reckon as ten bezants do not weigh one."* In an effort to end hyperinflation and regain control over the monetary system, the subsequent Ming dynasty ended the issue of paper money by 1455.

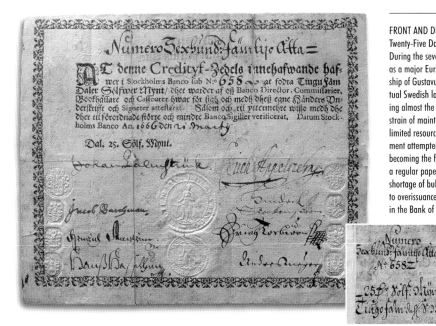

FRONT AND DETAIL OF BACK: Sweden, Bank of Sweden, Twenty-Five Daler Note, 1666
During the seventeenth century, Sweden established itself as a major European power under the dynamic leadership of Gustavus Adolphus. The Baltic Sea became a virtual Swedish lake with Swedish possessions encompassing almost the entire eastern and southern coasts. The strain of maintaining such an empire stretched Sweden's limited resources to the utmost. The Swedish government attempted to alleviate its monetary problems by becoming the first European country to experiment with a regular paper currency, mainly due to Sweden's chronic shortage of bullion. The experiment was short-lived due to overissuance of the notes and lack of public confidence in the Bank of Stockholm.

In Europe, Stockholm Banco, a predecessor of the Bank of Sweden, issued the first banknotes in 1660. These banknotes became popular very quickly simply because they were much easier to carry than the large copper daler "coins" then current; the largest measured up to two feet long and weighed sixty pounds! And whereas the daler coins had to be transported by horse and cart to make large payments, these banknotes could be sent in an envelope.

Paper money also simplified the operation and control of the monetary system. When using coinage whose value was based on its metallic content, any significant change in the value of the metal could cause the existing coins to become more valuable than their stated denomination. As a result, people would melt down the coins in order to sell the metal for a profit. This situation was particularly true of low-value metals such as copper, but could also occur with silver or gold—the resulting shortage of money could only be solved by replacing the coins with banknotes.

Unfortunately, the Stockholms Banco began to issue too many notes. When the bank ran out of copper to redeem its notes in 1664, the public's confidence in paper currency eroded. By the end of the year the bank had suspended operations and was reorganized, with the government and Riksdag (Swedish Parliament) forced to take over. Outstanding loans were reduced and notes exchanged for coins. The bank again issued notes in 1666 based on silver dalers instead of copper in order to facilitate the redemption of the older copper backed notes. The liquidation of the bank was completed in 1667.

Massachusetts Bay Colony, Twenty Shillings Bill of Credit, 1690
The Massachusetts Bay Colony was the first government in the Western world to issue paper money. It did so in response to an emergency that occurred during the first of the French & Indian Wars, known as King William's War to the English colonists, when the Massachusetts General Assembly was unable to pay its colonial soldiers after a failed invasion of Canada. The financial experiment was successful and paved the way for the introduction of paper money throughout the American colonies. Interestingly, this note, in common with all other known examples, was originally issued as two shillings six pence, and was subsequently illegally "raised" in value to twenty shillings. This illegal raise highlights one of the perennial problems with paper currency—counterfeiting.

Other European nations went through similar experiences during the late seventeenth and early eighteenth centuries. In many cases the experience so traumatized the nations involved that the use of paper money was delayed for many decades. Other countries, such as England, learned through the experiences of others and were able to introduce paper money as a permanent feature of their currency. In 1694 the Bank of England issued the first permanently circulating banknotes.

It was in the English colonies where paper money found its most enthusiastic supporters—and where the look and form of modern paper money was developed. The American colonists had no ready sources for gold or silver; nor could they get sufficient money for their needs from England, so paper money became an attractive alternative. Massachusetts, the largest and most economically developed of the colonies, led the way with the introduction of the first government-backed paper money in the Western world in 1690. By the 1750s every colony was using paper money, and paper had become a mainstay of the colonial economies.

By the second half of the nineteenth century, the United States was producing the finest bank notes in the world, as well as one of the most stable and secure paper currencies. American paper money became the model for many countries introducing paper for the first time. American concepts of how paper money should look also became the accepted standard for most of the world.

With the emergence of the United States as the world's leading economic power in the twentieth century, American paper money began a deliberate shift to more standardized and formal designs. These designs were intended to make the notes more recognizable and promote an image of stability and consistency that would ease their circulation worldwide. The result has been a relative stagnation of

American paper money design, which has become increasingly evident over the last forty years, as new technologies have revolutionized the look of paper currencies in the rest of the world, through the use of new colors, printing techniques, and even materials.

The use of new manufacturing and printing techniques has revolutionized the look and feel of paper money in recent decades. "Paper" money has traditionally been made of just that, paper. The earliest Chinese notes were made of paper produced from mulberry bark, which gives the notes their distinctive coloration. Since then, most bank notes have been made of heavy wood pulp-based paper, sometimes mixed with linen, cotton, or other textile fibers. Since the late 1980s, some countries, including Mexico and Australia, have begun to produce polymer banknotes made from a form of plastic. This new material has been developed in order to improve wear and tear (polymer notes last about four times longer than traditional paper notes), and to improve security for the notes. Polymer permits the inclusion of small transparent windows in the notes as a security feature that is very difficult to reproduce using common counterfeiting techniques. When combined with improvements and innovations in inks, such as the introduction of color shifting inks, the result is a new look and feel to banknotes that is revolutionizing modern "paper" money.

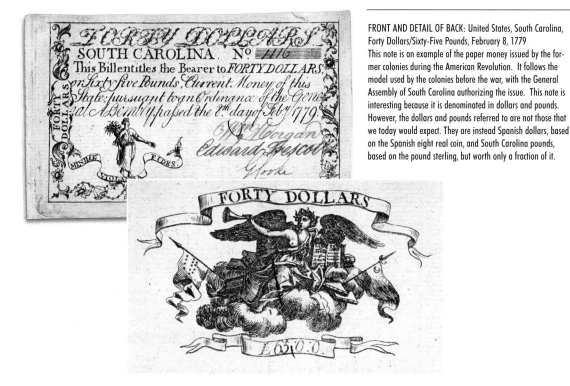

FRONT AND DETAIL OF BACK: United States, South Carolina, Forty Dollars/Sixty-Five Pounds, February 8, 1779
This note is an example of the paper money issued by the former colonies during the American Revolution. It follows the model used by the colonies before the war, with the General Assembly of South Carolina authorizing the issue. This note is interesting because it is denominated in dollars and pounds. However, the dollars and pounds referred to are not those that we today would expect. They are instead Spanish dollars, based on the Spanish eight real coin, and South Carolina pounds, based on the pound sterling, but worth only a fraction of it.

WESTERN EUROPE

The early history of money in the Mediterranean world begins with the Greek coinage tradition, invented by the Lydians in central Asia Minor. In the hands of the ancient Greeks, coins soon evolved into the first "world currency" for foreign exchange (in fact, the Greeks were so enthusiastic about coinage that they have given their name to the western coinage tradition). The Western monetary tradition was inherited by the Romans from the Greeks during the third century BC, and was changed forever by them as they extended the forms and types of coinage. The Romans turned coinage into an unparalleled medium for state propaganda—at a time when there were few forms of mass media, coinage had the greatest audience and dissemination.

Europe's political and economic fragmentation after the fall of the Roman Empire led to the development of a diversity of coinages with related denominational terms—such as the English pound/shilling/penny system, which corresponds to the French livre/sou/denier system—but with widely varying values. The relative values of the different currencies depended on the strength of the regional economies. At the end of the medieval period, Roman

OPPOSITE: Austria, Privilegirte Oesterreichische National Bank, Ten Gulden, January 15, 1863
This Austrian 10-gulden note of 1863 displays an image of a miner flanked by a shepherdess and a harvester. This image was designed to convey a sense of industry and peace, two elements necessary for a stable economy and monetary system. The scene is surmounted by the Hapsburg Imperial Eagle, suggesting the source of the peace and stability in the image below.

France, Louis XVI, Gold Two Louis d'Or, 1786
This coin is a good example of the coinage issued by the French monarchy on the eve of the French Revolution. It features a bust of Louis XVI with his titles in Latin (Louis XVI, King of France and Navarre by the Grace of God). The reverse of the coin features the arms of France and Navarre and a Latin legend (Christ reigns, conquers, and rules).

coinage was "rediscovered." It would have a profound effect on the Renaissance as the European economy revived, and the demand for a wider range of denominations and more politically sophisticated and aesthetically pleasing designs increased.

Modern European coinage begins at the end of the fifteenth century, with the discovery of extensive new sources of bullion in the New World and in central Europe. The flood of new gold and silver into the European economy began an economic boom and enabled the introduction of new, larger denominations of money to handle the increased volume of trade. During the fifteenth and sixteenth centuries, machines such as the drop press, the screw press, the rocker press, and the roller press were invented to replace the hand-held hammer as a means to create struck coins faster and with more precision. The introduction of steam-powered coin presses by Matthew Boulton and James Watt in the late eighteenth century allowed for further increases in speed, precision, and size in the production of coins. These advances in coining technology resulted in the coinages of today—machine struck,

France, Napoleon I, Silver 5 Francs, 1810
French coinage from the Revolution through the Napoleonic era reflected the rapid political changes that occurred. Republican imagery replaced the portrait of the King and the French people were recognized as the rulers of France. After Napoleon's coup, French coinage continued to reflect political changes, as Napoleon's title evolved from First Consul of the French Republic to Emperor of France. The model chosen for all of these changes was the coinage of the ancient Roman Republic and early Empire—on this piece Napoleon is depicted exactly as a Roman emperor, complete with the laurel wreath worn by the ancient emperors.

with perfectly round, milled edges, each an almost exact copy of the next. These advances also set the stage for the adoption of Western concepts of currency worldwide.

Paper money in Europe began with the Swedish Stockholm Banco, which issued Europe's first circulating banknotes in 1661. Despite the failure of this first experiment, paper money became increasingly common in Europe over the course of the eighteenth century. By the middle of the nineteenth century, paper money was widely accepted and used by a majority of people. The Bank of England has the longest continuous history of paper currency issuance, starting in 1694 and continuing to the present.

In the 1860s, France began an economic and diplomatic initiative that resulted in the development of the Latin Monetary Union. The Latin Monetary Union was an organization made up of various nations interested in improving trade through the creation of a single standard for member nations' gold and silver coinage. World War I finally ended this experiment, which had only limited success with the creation of a single standard for gold coins. The economic chaos of the 1920s in Europe, coupled with the onset of the Great Depression, made

European Union, France, Copper-Nickel Outer Part, Nickel-Brass Inner Part Two Euro, 1999
Euro coinage was introduced in certain countries alongside their national coinages before the 2002 replacement of all member nations' currencies. France issued this two-euro coin in 1999, when the exchange rate of euros to each member's national currency was irrevocably fixed. Euro coinage has a common obverse design for all of the denominations while the reverse design is chosen by the individual nations. Thus all two-euro coins are bimetallic, regardless of the issuing nation, and the obverse of all two-euro coins shares the same large two-euro legend with a map of Europe. A tree appears on the reverse of this coin, symbolizing life, continuity, and growth. It is contained in a hexagon and is surrounded by the motto of the French Republic, "Liberté, Egalité, Fraternité." This design also appears on the French one-euro coin.

further progress impossible until after World War II.

The devastation caused by World War II created a desire in many Europeans for a pan-European union, which would ideally prevent such a catastrophic war from happening ever again. Western Europe began to experiment with ideas for economic, political, and monetary union as early as the 1950s. Early initiatives included the creation of the ECU, which was a composite monetary unit consisting of a basket of European Community currencies that served as the predecessor to the euro.

In 2002, despite ongoing concerns over the submergence of national sovereignty and identity, the dream of a unified European currency finally became a reality, when twelve of the then fifteen member nations of the European Union adopted the euro as their only currency. The members of the European Union that chose to adopt the euro were required to cease using their national currencies within a year of the euro's introduction. The new monetary system uses the old national mints to produce the new coinage with a standard obverse design for all of the coins, but with individual national designs for the reverse of the coins. These national designs can only be altered every five years in order to maintain some consistency in the coinage. The design of euro banknotes is based on a bridge theme, different for each denomination, symbolizing the unification of Europe through the breaking down of economic barriers among member nations. The issuing nation can only be identified by the use of a letter at the start of the note's serial number.

So far, fifteen European nations have adopted euros, with the possibility that other members of the European Union (now up to twenty-five nations, with more soon to follow) may adopt the euro as well. Interestingly, several nations have refused to adopt the euro, most notably the United Kingdom and Denmark, despite meeting the necessary requirements. Both of these nations continue to use their own national currencies and will likely do so for the foreseeable future.

United Kingdom, Queen Elizabeth II, Bimetallic Two Pounds, 1998
In 1997, Great Britain introduced a new bimetallic two-pound coin with the portrait of Queen Elizabeth II on the obverse (as with all English coinage) and a Celtic-inspired geometric design on the reverse. Despite being one of the core members of the European Union, Great Britain has refused to join the euro community. Like Denmark, Great Britain has retained its national coinage.

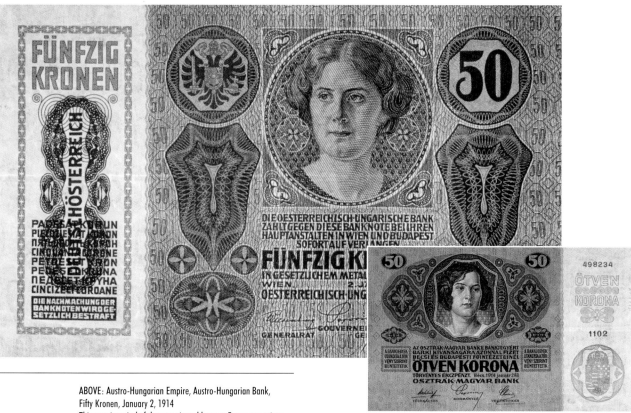

ABOVE: Austro-Hungarian Empire, Austro-Hungarian Bank, Fifty Kronen, January 2, 1914
This note is typical of the notes issued by most European nations on the eve of World War I. It has an elaborate multi-colored design printed on both sides, with one side in German (for Austria) and the other side printed in Hungarian—in recognition of the growing importance of nationalism in European politics, particularly in Central and Eastern Europe. The growth of nationalism among minorities within the European empires was a major cause of World War I.

RIGHT: United Kingdom, George III, Bronze Penny, 1806
This coin is typical of the types issued during the latter part of the reign of George III. It has a bust of George III on the obverse, while the reverse has an allegorical image of Britannia with trident, olive branch, and shield. In the background is a ship, symbolic of English naval power.

ABOVE: Austria, Privilegirte Oesterreichische National Bank, Five Gulden, March 1, 1859

Because of its dependency on banknotes to support state finances, Austria continued to be a leader in developing new anticounterfeiting techniques during the early nineteenth century. In order to stabilize an economy disrupted by two decades of war, Austria founded the Privilegirte Oesterreichische National Bank in 1816 as an independent stock-holding company, modeled on the French and English central banks, with the right to issue banknotes. The bank was able to stabilize the monetary system and produced notes such as this five-gulden note of 1859.

LEFT: Austria, Wiener-Stadt-Banco, Two Gulden, January 1, 1880

Austria began issuing paper money in 1762 as a means to offset state debts incurred during the frequent wars of the period. The Wiener-Stadt-Banco issued the first Austrian banknotes and continued to do so until 1806. At the time this note was issued in 1800, there were approximately twenty countries around the world using paper money issued by private issuers, state banks, or the governments themselves. This note incorporates the latest anticounterfeiting devices known to that date—watermarked paper, embossed coats of arms, multiple hand-signatures and serial numbers, fine engraving of details, and two different-colored inks.

France, Banque de France, Fifty Francs, April 9, 1927
Germany and France pioneered the use of the four-color printing process on banknotes during the latter part of the nineteenth century. France, in particular, used colors to produce some of the most striking notes of the early twentieth century, when most countries continued to produce monochromatic or, at most, two-color banknotes. More reminiscent of a painting than a piece of money, this fifty-franc note has a luxuriant use of colors in its design.

UPPER: France, Banque de France, Fifty Francs, December 30, 1937
This note is typical of French paper money of the period, issued both at home and in French colonies. Bright colors are used to highlight a scene designed to represent the culture and history of the country. In this case, ancient Greek gods are displayed—Mercury on the front and Ceres on the back. Notes issued for the French colonies in Africa and the Pacific had similar designs using local motifs for inspiration, often with a paternalistic acknowledgement of the benefits of French control in the territories.

LOWER: France, Banque de France, Ten Francs, March 5, 1970
After World War II, French banknotes began to celebrate the accomplishments of famous Frenchmen. This ten-franc note features Francois Voltaire (1694–1778), the French philosopher and writer, with the Tuileries Palace in the background. The back of the franc has a slightly different image of Voltaire facing in the opposite direction, with the Chateau de Cirey in the background. French banknotes continued to use the almost mirror image of individuals on both sides until their replacement by the euro in 2002.

Sweden, Sveriges Riksbank, Twenty Kronor, 1996
During the 1660s, Sweden was the first European nation to experiment with paper money. After that traumatic experience, confidence in paper money was shaken to the point that it would be another thirty years before Sweden again issued paper money—in 1701, to be exact. That year, Sweden issued paper money only because of a national financial emergency: the start of the Great Northern War (1700–1721). The front of this note features Selma Lagerlof (1858–1940), Swedish novelist and the first woman to win the Nobel Prize for literature. The back of the note displays a scene from one of Lagerlof's children's books.

UPPER: Sweden, Sveriges Riksbank, Fifty Kronor, 1997
The Swedish 50-kronor note of the 1997 series features Jenny Lind (1820–1887),
a famous singer known as the "Swedish Nightingale." The vignette to the right of
the note displays the old Stockholm Opera House, where Jenny Lind made her last
appearance in Sweden in 1848. The back of the note has a violin in front of a
musical score and an abstract design.

LOWER: Sweden, Sveriges Riksbank, One Hundred Kronor, 2001
The Swedish 100-hundred kronor note features Carl von Linne (1707–1778),
known in English as Charles Linnaeus, the naturalist who created the modern system for the classification of animals and plants into families and species. The front
also has images of several plants taken from Linnaeus' works. The back of the
note features renderings of scientific photographs of various natural phenomena,
such as the pollination of a plant.

03G100847

03G1008479

BANQUE NATIONALE SUISSE
BANCA NAZIONALE SVIZZERA

Switzerland, Banque Nationale Suisse, Twenty Swiss Francs, October 1, 1996
The front of the Swiss 20-franc note features a portrait of Arthur Honegger
(1892–1955), a famous Swiss composer. The back of the note features a collage of elements important in Honegger's work—parts of different instruments, representations of
technology, which played an important part in the background of his compositions, and
parts of a musical score.

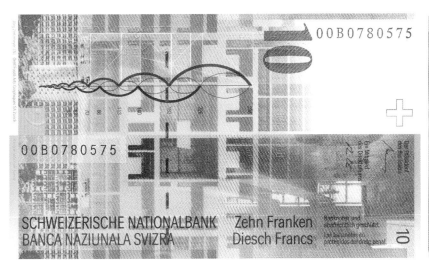

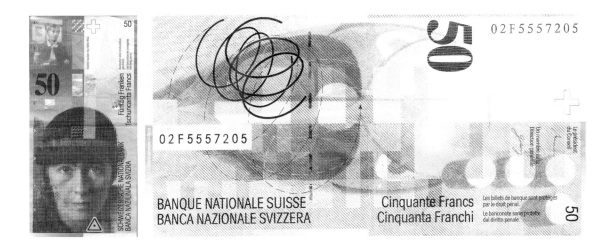

UPPER: Switzerland, Banque Nationale Suisse, Ten Swiss Francs, April 8, 1997
The front of the Swiss 10-franc note features a portrait of Charles Edouard Jenneret, better known as Le Corbusier (1887–1965), an influential designer and architect, on a multi-hued background. The back of the note displays a collage of some of the buildings that Le Corbusier built during his career.

LOWER: Switzerland, Banque Nationale Suisse, Fifty Swiss Francs, October 3, 1995
The front of the Swiss 50-franc note features a portrait of Sophie Taeuber-Arp (1889–1943), an abstract artist who became very influential in modern art. The back of the note has a composite image of several of Taeuber-Arp's artwork in various media.

United Kingdom, Bank of England, Twenty Pounds, 1999

This 20-pound note has the portrait of Elizabeth II on the front. The back features Sir Edward Elgar (1857–1934), one of England's most famous composers. His *Enigma Variations*, which propelled him to fame, was first performed in 1899 at the Worcester Cathedral, which is the subject of the background vignette. An interesting fact about Bank of England notes is that all of its issues from 1694 (the date when the bank opened its doors and when it began to issue banknotes) on are still valid as currency at face value, much as all U.S. federal currency from 1861 on is still legal tender. Of course the collector value of most of these notes is well above what their face value is today.

UPPER: United Kingdom, Bank of England, Five Pounds, 2002
In 2002, the United Kingdom issued a new series of notes with enhanced security features and new back designs. This five-pound note features a portrait of Queen Elizabeth II on the front, in common with all British banknotes. The back of the note has an image of Elizabeth Fry (1780–1845), a Quaker philanthropist and social reformer best known for her successful support of prison reforms in England. The note's background vignette shows Elizabeth Fry reading to prisoners in Newgate Prison.

LOWER: United Kingdom, Bank of England, Ten Pounds, 2000
This 10-pound note displays Elizabeth II on the front. The back of the note features Charles Darwin (1809–1882), the famous English naturalist who developed the theory of evolution through natural selection. The background vignette is of the HMS Beagle (Darwin's ship), the flora and fauna he came across in his travels, and a magnifying glass.

UPPER: European Union, Germany, One Hundred Euro, 2002
The 100-hundred euro banknote features Baroque and Rococo architecture for the front and back.

LOWER: European Union, Belgium, Fifty Euro, 2002
The 50-euro note has Renaissance architecture for its theme. Euro notes feature five variant initials for the European Central Bank covering the eleven official languages of the European Union. The word "euro" is also spelled out in the Latin and Greek alphabets.

LEFT: European Union, Austria, Five Euro, 2002
The year 2002 marked an epoch-making event in European history—the introduction of the euro as the sole legal-tender currency of twelve independent European countries. This event marked the final stage of a series of agreements and economic and political adjustments that allowed for the creation of a single monetary unit, despite the historical rivalries of the nations involved. The euro was designed to provide an economically unifying currency that would strengthen the member nations' economies, both internally and externally. All euro banknote denominations share a common design, regardless of the issuing nation, and are exchangeable across all the member nations. The only distinguishing feature on the notes is the designation letter at the start of the serial number that identifies the issuing nation. The five-euro note features a Roman archway on the front and a Roman aqueduct on the back.

LEFT: European Union, Germany, Ten Euro, 2002
All euro banknotes share a common theme regardless of their denomination—the fronts depict various types of archways and windows along with the flag of the European Union, while the backs display different styles of bridges and a map of Europe. The 10-euro note has a Romanesque theme for the archway on the front and a bridge on the back.

LEFT: European Union, The Netherlands, Twenty Euro, 2002
The 20-euro note has Gothic architecture as its theme, with Gothic-style stained windows on the front. The back has a bridge with Gothic arches. Each member nation of the euro-using nations has a letter code in front of the serial number that identifies the notes produced in that country: L for Finland, M for Portugal, N for Austria, P for The Netherlands, S for Italy, T for Ireland, U for France, V for Spain, X for Germany, Y for Greece, and Z for Belgium.

LEFT: European Union, Spain, Nordic Gold Fifty Euro Cents, 1999
The Spanish 50-euro cent coin, in common with the Spanish 20-cent and 10-cent pieces, features Miguel de Cervantes, the father of Spanish literature. Through the use of the reverse of the new euro coins, the member nations of the euro community have managed to maintain a monetary outlet for individual expressions of national pride and cultural accomplishment. The composition alloy of this coin is known as Nordic Gold—it is an alloy of copper, aluminum, zinc, and tin.

EASTERN EUROPE

*A*lthough the iron curtain is no more, the modern countries of Eastern Europe do not currently belong to the European Union; hence, the euro is nowhere to be found in these former Soviet-bloc countries—at least not on the open market. Before the Soviet occupation effectively divided the European continent, however, the currencies of these regions shared a history dating back to the fifteenth century.

It was the age of Christopher Columbus, whose epic journeys across the Atlantic led to the birth of the Spanish Empire. The New World yielded extensive new sources of bullion, as did central Europe. The flood of new gold and silver into the European markets began an economic boom; it also enabled the introduction of new larger denominations of money to handle the increased volume of trade. The modernization of coining techniques during the fifteenth and sixteenth centuries occurred in many of the western portions of this region, such as Poland, Bohemia, and Hungary, but was delayed in Russia and the Balkans.

DETAIL OF: Estonia, 500 Marka, 1923
With the end of World War I, Estonia, along with Latvia and Lithuania, became independent from the Russian Empire for the first time in centuries. This was not to last for long, however, as the Soviet Union invaded the three Baltic nations as part of their conquest of eastern Poland, in conjunction, with Nazi Germany at the start of WWII.

Russia, Nicholas II, Silver Commemorative Ruble, 1913
This coin celebrates the 300th anniversary of Romanov rule in Russia with an interesting image of Nicholas II next to Michael Romanov, the founder of the dynasty. Within four years Nicholas II and his family would be dead, casualties of the Russian Revolution that led to the establishment of the Soviet Union.

With the accession of Peter the Great in Russia, that country began to take the lead in matters political as well as economic in Eastern Europe. Russia's coinage was modernized virtually overnight. By the early nineteenth century, Russia dominated the region with modern machine-made coins. Then, in 1917, a watershed event in the money of the region occurred: the Russian Revolution. Suddenly, new imagery and messages designed to inspire Communist solidarity and internationalism were the rule of the day, with each autonomous Soviet Republic issuing a widely diversified range of money, mostly in the form of paper notes. By the mid-1920s, with the end of the Russian Civil War, a unified national currency reasserted itself. This currency used striking imagery glorifying the proletarian and internationalist ideals of the Revolution. In the aftermath of World War II, there was a resurgence of nationalism in the Soviet-bloc nations. This nationalistic fervor had a moribund effect on the artistic quality of currency designs in Eastern Europe. The imagery on coinage and paper money settled down to official forms emphasizing state seals and portraits of past or current leaders.

With the fall of the Soviet Union in the early 1990s, the currency of Eastern Europe experienced a brilliant flowering of artistic designs and imagery. Each nation of the former Soviet Union celebrated its freedom from the stifling effects of Communism and foreign domination. Nations long submerged in Soviet repression issued new currency celebrating the old national heroes and the achievements of their pre-Soviet leaders and cultural icons. There was also a revival of the use of religious symbolism in currency design. Poland and the Czech Republic led the way in the issuance of new and interesting money. This initial trend was somewhat dampened as economic reality set in, and created numerous changes in the money of the region at the dawn of the twenty-first century. Over the last few years, with the successful establishment of the euro as the currency of most of Western Europe, many of the former Soviet-bloc nations have begun to join the European Union (EU). Several have also applied for membership in the euro community, despite the requirements of membership (involving the opening of markets long closed to the

USSR, Lenin, Gold Ten Rubles, 1923
As the Soviet Union became more stable, it began to issue coinage in its own name. The Soviet economy was isolated from that of the rest of the world—for ideological reasons and also as a punishment for not honoring the international debts of the Imperial Russian government. In order to trade internationally, the Soviet Union created the so-called chervonetz trade coinage in gold and silver, which could be exchanged at bullion value. The imagery on these coins celebrated the ideals of Communism, with images such as this powerful-looking traditional farmer, gazing toward the modern factories in the distance.

outside world and the imposition of economic reforms). The following former Soviet-bloc countries joined the European Union in 2004: Latvia, Lithuania, Slovakia, the Czech Republic, Estonia, Cyprus, Slovenia, Poland, and Hungary. Bulgaria, Turkey, Croatia, and Romania are currently applying to join the EU, with Romania and Bulgaria due to join in 2007. The adoption of the euro for these countries will take more time and is dependent on each country's ability to meet the stringent prerequirements for entry. Estonia is due to be the first new member of the euro community in 2006, followed tentatively by Cyprus and Lithuania in 2007. As this process continues, the former diversity of European currency will be replaced by monetary unity. Hopefully, aesthetic conformity will not fully supplant the interesting and historic national variations in European money.

USSR, Leonid Brezhnev, Copper-Nickel Ruble, 1970
This coin commemorates the one-hundredth anniversary of Lenin's birth. During World War II, Soviet propaganda heavily influenced currency design, which then featured interesting patriotic and historical images. These images were designed to inspire the common citizen with nationalistic zeal to fight the Germans. Unfortunately, regular coinage was not affected. After the war, coinage design settled into official designs and patterns that became increasingly devoid of artistic quality, except for occasional commemorative issues. This is a good example of the bland coinage typical of the Soviet period.

Greece, Bank of Greece, 1000 Drachmai, January 1, 1939
This note was issued in Greece just prior to the start of World War II. The front of the note displays a young woman in traditional Greek clothing. The reverse features the head of Athena wearing a crown, with the Sphinx flanked by two winged horses, next to an image of the Athenian Acropolis, in which the upper portion of the Parthenon is visible.

Estonia, 500 Marka, 1923
With the end of World War I, Estonia, along with Latvia and Lithuania, became independent from the Russian Empire for the first time in centuries. This was not to last for long, however, as the Soviet Union invaded the three Baltic nations as part of their conquest of eastern Poland in conjunction with Nazi Germany at the start of World War II. With the end of that war, Estonia, Lithuania, and Latvia were reabsorbed and remained part of the Soviet Union until its collapse in the early 1990s. The countries are once again independent. This note displays a castle built by the Teutonic knights on the front.

Bulgaria, One Hundred Leva Srebro, 1904

This note, issued in Bulgaria in 1904, is one of the few notes of its time to display bright colors. The front of the note shows a geometric design, along with the national coat of arms, while the back shows another geometric design in multiple colors, designed to foil counterfeiters.

BELOW: Bulgaria, Bronze Five Stotinki, 1990
This Bulgarian coin is typical of the coinage of the
Soviet-bloc nations—artistry was sacrificed in favor
of pure functionality. After the collapse of the Soviet
Union, nearly all of the former Soviet satellite
nations issued new money with images evoking
their national, non-Communist past.

Bulgaria, Bulgarian Treasury, 1000 Leva Zlatni, 1920
This 1000—leva zlatni note displays the Bulgarian penchant for geometric design, just as
does the 100—leva srebro note of 1904. In addition to the national coat of arms, the geometric pattern and various cartouches for the text elements create a unique design.

Poland, Narodowy Bank Polski (National Bank of Poland), Ten Zloty, March 25, 1994
In January of 1995, Poland issued a new series of banknotes to replace its previous issues, at the rate of 10,000 old
zloty for one new zloty. The new series focuses on famous Polish hero-kings of the past. The front of the Polish ten-
zloty note features Mieszko I (935–932 AD), the first Duke of the Polans, a Slavic tribe that gave its name to the future
Polish nation. The back of the note shows an image of a silver denar from Mieszko's reign.

Poland, Narodowy Bank Polski (National Bank of Poland), Bimetallic Two Zloty, 2005
This Polish coin commemorates Pope John Paul II (1920–2005), a Polish national hero and world figure. The reverse features a traditional Polish heraldic eagle, which has been used in Poland for centuries.

Poland, Narodowy Bank Polski (National Bank of Poland), Twenty Zloty, March 25, 1994
The Polish 20-zloty note features the portrait of Boleslaw I Chrobry (966–1025), son of Mieszko I. Boleslaw founded the Polish kingdom in 1025, just before his death that same year. The back of the note displays a silver denar from Boleslaw's reign.

Poland, Narodowy Bank Polski (National Bank of Poland), Fifty Zloty, March 25, 1994
The front of the Polish 50-zloty note features Kazimierz III Wielki (1310–1370), known in English as Casimir the
Great. Casimir was a great reformer and leader who was able to double the size and increase the prosperity of his
country. The back of the note has a crowned eagle taken from one of Casimir's thrones, along with an orb and a
scepter, symbols of his power. The background of the note features medieval views of Cracow and Kazimierz.

Poland, Narodowy Bank Polski (National Bank of Poland), One Hundred Zloty, March 25, 1994
The front of this note has a portrait of Wladyslaw II Jagiello (ca. 1351–1434), Grand Duke of Lithuania who became King of Poland after converting to Christianity in 1386. His reign is remembered as a golden reign era in Polish history. The back of the note features the Polish eagle on a shield with crossed swords and a helmet below. An image of the Teutonic knights' castle of Malbork is visible in the background.

ABOVE: Russia, Russian Bank, 1000 Rubles, January 2, 2001
The 1000-ruble note depicts a monument to Prince Yaroslav the
Wise (ca. 978–1054), the prince of Kiev who managed to unite
the principalities of Novgorod and Kiev, marking the high point
of the Kievan Rus culture and military power. The back of the
note features the Church of the Precursor in Yaroslavl.

RIGHT: Russia, Peter the Great, Silver Ruble, 1704
Peter the Great modernized the Russian monetary system, along with
almost every other part of Russian public life and government. This
coin is an early example of Peter's reformed coinage—a silver ruble
struck with newly acquired mint machinery. The coin features an
armored bust of the young Tsar on the obverse and the Imperial
Russian eagle on the reverse. As was common for Russian coins of this
era, it is over-struck on a European thaler—the remains of the original design can be seen along the top half of the reverse of the coin.

БИЛЕТ БАНКА РОССИИ

ЗЯ 2244269

ЗЯ 2244269

500

500 500 500

ПОДДЕЛКА
БИЛЕТОВ
БАНКА РОССИИ
ПРЕСЛЕДУЕТСЯ
ПО ЗАКОНУ

АРХАНГЕЛЬСК

ПЯТЬСОТ РУБЛЕЙ

500 500

500

ПЯТЬСОТ РУБЛЕЙ

1997

ABOVE: Russia, Russian Bank, 500 Rubles, January 2, 1998
The front of the Russian 500-ruble note features a statue of
Peter the Great (1672–1725) with an image of the harbor of
Archangelsk in the background. Peter was arguably the greatest of the Russian Tsars. He reformed Russia and brought it
into the circle of European nations, in part through the encour-
agement of maritime trade. The back of the note shows an
image of the monastery on Solovetsky Island.

LEFT: Russia, Russian Bank, Bimetallic Ten Rubles, 2003
This coin is representative of the newest issues of Russian commemorative coinage. It is bimetallic, following trends in Europe and much
of the rest of the world. The coin is part of a series celebrating
ancient Russian towns. This coin features a view of Murom in central
Russia, with two coats of arms of the town above. The reverse of the
coin features the denomination and issue date of the coin.

20

The Hongkong and Shanghai Banking Cor

AH580864

Pr

TH憑

By 承

GE
HO
香

EAST ASIA

$\mathcal{A}$sia has been the crossroads for the exchange of ideas and goods ever since the beginnings of civilization in the four great "cradles" of the Nile river valley, the Fertile Crescent formed by the Tigris and Euphrates rivers, the Indus River, and the Yalu River in China. Displaying elements of all three major world monetary traditions, the modern currency of Asia reflects the diversity of its cultural origins. China retains the influence of its indigenous monetary tradition, as does India, while the Islamic monetary tradition is dominant in Central Asia.

After the late seventh-century BC invention of Chinese coinage by the kings of the Zhou State, the use of coinage spread and developed rapidly within the Chinese core regions. The unification of China under the Qin dynasty during the third century BC provided the impetus for the spread of the newly introduced ban liang cast coins. The ban liang became the prototype for the coinage of the Far East. An interesting feature of Chinese coinage is that their coins were cast, not struck, and that the Chinese used only base metals for their

China, Silver 10-Tael Ingot, Nineteenth Century
The Chinese government avoided striking coins in silver and gold until the 1890s. Previously silver was used in transactions either in the form of chop-marked (marks stamped into coins as verification of their silver content) foreign coins or silver ingots. These ingots took various forms depending on the tradition within each province.

DETAIL OF: Hong Kong, Hong Kong and Shanghai Banking Corporation Limited, Twenty Hong Kong Dollars, January 17, 2003
The Hong Kong and Shanghai Banking Corporation (HKSBC) issues this note. It features a lion's head on the front.

China, Ming Dynasty, Shih Tsu, Bronze Five Cash, 1644–1661
This coin represents the final basic type of Chinese round coinage. It has four characters on the obverse that identify the Emperor Shih Tsu and the denomination, and two on the reverse that identify the mint and/or the issuing agency. During the era of the Ming dynasty, different bureaus of the imperial government had the right to issue coinage. The square hole in the center was useful not only for stringing the coins, but was also important in preparing the coins for use: After casting they would be threaded onto square rods that would allow the edges of the coins to be filed smooth. Coins of this type became the model for coinage throughout East and Southeast Asia.

coins, such as copper, bronze, and iron. The final form of traditional Chinese coinage appeared during the Ming dynasty (1644–1911) with the introduction of characters on the back of the coins to identify the location of the mint and the government agency responsible for the coin's issue.

Starting with the Qin and Han dynasties, the development of a strong centralized government over a unified Chinese Empire formed a solid basis for the spread and diffusion of the Chinese monetary tradition. Later, during the golden age of the Tang dynasty, Chinese art, literature and currency flourished. The rulers of the Tang dynasty issued coins that became the basis for coinage systems throughout Southeast and Eastern Asia. Japan's coinage system began in 708 AD. The first Vietnamese coinage followed in 970 AD. Twenty-six years later, Korean coinage was introduced in 996 AD. All of these nations followed Chinese conventions in the use of metals in coins—silver and gold were almost never used in coinage. These elements were instead used in the form of ingots of various shapes and sizes.

The Chinese have the distinction of inventing the world's first paper money, which was introduced during the Tang dynasty in the seventh century in the form of privately issued notes. The first surviving specimens date from the fourteenth century and consist of large notes (15 inches x 10 inches) made from mulberry bark issued by the Chinese government. Marco Polo was the first Westerner to report on the use of paper money by the Chinese. One of these notes was the one-kuan note, which was issued during the Ming dynasty. Although rather unwieldy due to its size, the kuan was nonetheless elaborately illustrated, with a rendering of ten strings of copper coins in the note's center, surrounded by geometric designs and Chinese characters; each string was composed of one hundred copper coins. Alongside actual strings of copper coins and ingots of silver, notes like the kuan were used for centuries, despite problems with counterfeiting.

At the end of the nineteenth century, with the fall of the Japanese shogunate and the decline of the Chinese Empire, Western ideas of money took a firm hold in Eastern Asia. This resulted in an initial Western style of currency,

Japan, Tokugawa Shogunate, Gold Oban, 1860
The Japanese began the regular production of coinage during the eighth century AD. These Waido kaiho—"beginning treasure of the Wado period"—were based on Chinese coin types and remained in use until the late nineteenth century. Japan also used gold and silver as money in the form of ingots—this oban is an example of the largest and most impressive denomination. These "coins" were issued by individual Daimyo (provincial governors) during the Tokugawa shogunate (1603–1868) as gifts, payments, and marks of favor.

China, Nationalist Chinese Government, Silver One Dollar, 1932
This is a good example of the modern coins being struck in China before World War II. It follows the traditional dollar denomination, based on the Spanish dollar that had circulated in China for over two centuries. The first Western-style dollar coins were issued by Sun Yat Sen, the first president of the Chinese Republic, in 1912. This coin was issued by Chiang Kai-shek, the head of the Kuomintang party and President of Nationalist China. The Nationalist government was defeated by Mao Zedong's Communist Party in 1949 and retreated to Taiwan, where they remain today. The reverse of the coin features an image of ancient Chinese "spade" money.

which was increasingly "Orientalized" over time to reflect native traditions and culture. Coins of Western type were introduced with Western dates and often using the Western (Latin) alphabet and European-style portraits and imagery. Paper money followed the same pattern, with notes produced in France, Great Britain, or the United States, following the conventions used in the producing countries, with only minor concessions to the culture of the issuing nations.

Today, the currencies of twenty-first-century East Asian countries often celebrate native icons and indigenous flora and fauna. For example, the 2003 edition of Japan's 5000-yen banknote features both irises and nineteenth century novelist Ichiyo Higuchi. Regarded as Japan's first professional woman writer, Higuchi is also first woman to appear on a Japanese banknote since 1881. Japan has also reintroduced a hole into some of their coins in imitation of the traditional coinage of the region. That said, the currencies of Japan and other East Asian countries still adhere to the forms and concepts of the Western monetary tradition while introducing imagery from their own diverse cultural traditions.

UPPER: Indonesia, Bank of Indonesia, 2500 Rupiah, 1957
The front of this note features a scene from one of the several small islands that are home to the Komodo dragon, the largest lizard species on the planet—reaching up to ten feet in length. The back of the note displays a scene of an Indonesian village on the water.

LOWER: Indonesia, Bank of Indonesia, 500 Rupiah, 1982
The front of this note displays a man observing Amorphophallus titanum in bloom. Sumatra is famous for this flowering plant, the largest flower in the world. When fully open it is six feet tall and three feet in diameter. The flower opens only for two days before it withers away. Aside from its size, the Amorphophallus titanum is known for its smell—the odor of decaying carrion. The back of the note features an image of the Bank of Indonesia building.

Japan, Kanazawa Clan, One Hundred Mon,
Eighteenth–Nineteenth Century
Over 250 individual Japanese clans issued
paper money during the eighteenth and
nineteenth centuries. These notes were
backed by silver and issued because of a
shortage of official coinage. By the end of
the Tokugawa shogunate (1603–1868),
temples, townships, and other corporate
entities were also issuing similar notes.

UPPER: Japan, Imperial Government, One Yen, 1873
The yen was introduced in 1870 as the Japanese equivalent to the silver dollar. This note was the first of the Western-style notes issued in Japan. The Continental Bank Note Company of New York, New York produced it. The vignettes on the note celebrate the defeat of attempted Mongol invasions by Japanese samurai, with the aid of the kamikaze or "divine wind" during the late thirteenth century.

LOWER: Japan, Imperial Government, One Yen, 1877
This one-yen note is interesting for its combination of Japanese and Western imagery on a note. The front of the note has two sailors wearing Western-style clothing and standing on a Western type of ship. The reverse has an image of an accountant in traditional clothing with an abacus.

UPPER: Japan, Bank of Japan, 1000 Yen, 2004
In 2004, the Bank of Japan issued a new series of notes replacing the then current series. The front of the 1000-yen note features a portrait of Hideyo Noguchi (1876–1928), a famous Japanese bacteriologist who discovered the bacterial agent that causes syphilis in 1911. The back of the note displays Mount Fuji with cherry blossoms in the foreground.

LOWER: Japan, Bank of Japan, 2000 Yen, 2004
The 2000-yen note features an image of the famous Shureimon Gate, the second of Shuri Castle's gates built during the sixteenth century. At one time the political center of Okinawa, Shuri Castle is now a famous landmark. The back of the note displays a scene from the Tale of Genji with a portrait of its author Murasaki Shikibu (ca. 976–ca. 1031), a famous female Japanese author.

UPPER: Japan, Bank of Japan, 5000 Yen, 2004
The 5000-yen note displays a portrait of Ichiyo Higuchi (1872–1896), a famous Japanese novelist who tragically died young of tuberculosis. The back of the note has an image of irises taken from an artwork by Korin Ogata (1658–1716).

LOWER: Japan, Bank of Japan, 10,000 Yen, 1984
The 10,000-yen note displays a portrait of Yukichi Fukuzawa (1835–1901), founder of Keio University and one of the first Japanese experts on the West. The back of the note features the statue of a phoenix in Kyoto's Byodoin Temple, which dates from the eleventh century.

ZHONGGUO RENMIN YINH

ABOVE: China, People's Bank of China, Two Yuan, 1990
The two-yuan Chinese note features an image of two happy young
Uyghurs in traditional costume. The Uyghurs are a Turkic people living
in China's westernmost province, Xinjiang Uyghur Autonomous Region.
The back of the note displays a rocky outcrop in rough seas.

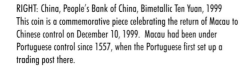

RIGHT: China, People's Bank of China, Bimetallic Ten Yuan, 1999
This coin is a commemorative piece celebrating the return of Macau to
Chinese control on December 10, 1999. Macau had been under
Portuguese control since 1557, when the Portuguese first set up a
trading post there.

LEFT: China, People's Bank of China, Five Yuan, 1999
The five-yuan note features a portrait of Mao Zedong (1893–1976), Communist China's founder and revolutionary leader. The back of the note has an image from a painting of the Yangtze River gorge.

LEFT: China, People's Bank of China, Ten Yuan, 1999
The Chinese 10-yuan note also features a portrait of Mao Zedong (1893–1976), Communist China's founder and revolutionary leader. The back of the note displays an image of a river.

LEFT: China, People's Bank of China, One Hundred Yuan, 1999
The Chinese 100-yuan note also features a portrait of Mao Zedong. The back of the note has an image of the Great Hall of the People in Beijing, the meeting place of the Chinese Parliament, also known as the Hall of 10,000 because it can seat all 10,000 parliament members.

Hong Kong, Government of the Hong Kong Special Administrative Region, Ten Hong Kong Dollars, January 1, 2003
This note is issued by the Government of the Hong Kong Special Administrative Region, a special subunit of the Chinese government in which certain free-market practices and special economic incentives are allowed—unlike in the rest of China. Hong Kong was a British Crown Colony from 1842 until 1997, when it reverted to Chinese control. This note features purple as its dominant color and has geometric designs on both sides.

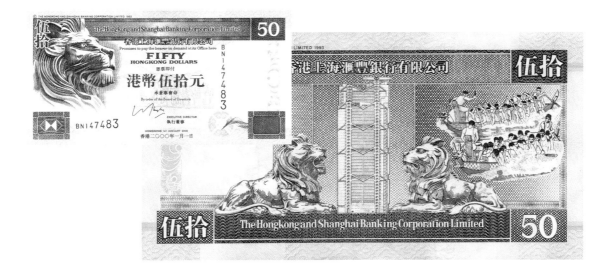

UPPER: Hong Kong, Hong Kong and Shanghai Banking Corporation Limited, Twenty Hong Kong Dollars, January 17, 2003
The Hong Kong and Shanghai Banking Corporation (HKSBC) issues this note. It features a lion's head on the front, and an elevated view of Hong Kong harbor with a railway in the foreground on the back.

LOWER: Hong Kong, Hong Kong and Shanghai Banking Corporation Limited, Fifty Hong Kong Dollars, January 1, 2000
Another note issued by HKSBC, this 50 Hong Kong–dollar note features a lion's head on the front with a view of Hong Kong. On the back the note features two lions flanking a large modernistic tower, with an image of a Chinese canoe race on the upper right.

Malaysia, Bank Negara Malaysia, One Ringgit, 2000
The front of all of the Malaysian banknotes features a portrait of Tuanku Abdul Rahman (1895–1960), the first Seri Paduka Baginda Yang di-Pertuan Agong (roughly equivalent to King) of independent Malaysia and a supporter of Parliamentary democracy in his country. The back of the one-ringgit note has an image of a Malaysian kite, the beach, Mount Kinabalu, and the pinnacles of Gunung Api, located in Mulu National Park.

UPPER: Malaysia, Bank Negara Malaysia, Two Ringgits, 1996
The front of all of the Malaysian banknotes features a portrait of Tuanku Abdul Rahman (1895–1960), the first Seri Paduka Baginda Yang di-Pertuan Agong (roughly equivalent to King) of independent Malaysia and a supporter of Parliamentary democracy in his country. The back of the two-ringgit note has a modern telecommunication network as the background motif.

LOWER: Malaysia, Bank Negara Malaysia, Five Ringgits, 1999
The front of all of the Malaysian banknotes features a portrait of Tuanku Abdul Rahman (1895–1960), the first Seri Paduka Baginda Yang di-Pertuan Agong (roughly equivalent to King) of independent Malaysia and a supporter of Parliamentary democracy in his country. The back of the five-ringgit note displays the Kuala Lumpur International Airport, the Petronas Twin Towers, and a geographical map with symbols representing the location of Putrajaya and Cyberjaya.

Malaysia, Bank Negara Malaysia, Ten Ringgits, 1998
The front of all of the Malaysian banknotes features a portrait of Tuanku Abdul
Rahman (1895–1960), the first Seri Paduka Baginda Yang di-Pertuan Agong (roughly equivalent to King) of independent Malaysia and a supporter of Parliamentary
democracy in his country. The back of the 10-ringgit note displays a jet airliner, a
train, and a container ship representing Malayasia's transportation system.

UPPER: Malaysia, Bank Negara Malaysia, Fifty Ringgits, 1998
The front of all of the Malaysian banknotes features a portrait of Tuanku Abdul Rahman (1895–1960), the first Seri Paduka Baginda Yang di-Pertuan Agong (roughly equivalent to King) of independent Malaysia and a supporter of Parliamentary democracy in his country. The back of the 50-ringgit note features an oil-drilling platform and a well-head control valve.

LOWER: Malaysia, Bank Negara Malaysia, One Hundred Ringgits, 1998
The front of all of the Malaysian banknotes features a portrait of Tuanku Abdul Rahman (1895–1960), the first Seri Paduka Baginda Yang di-Pertuan Agong (roughly equivalent to King) of independent Malaysia and a supporter of Parliamentary democracy in his country. The back of the 100-ringgit note displays an automobile assembly line and a detailed view of a Proton car engine.

INDIAN SUBCONTINENT AND SOUTHEAST ASIA

*I*ndia has a native coin tradition that dates back to at least the sixth century BC, before the conquests of Alexander the Great and his successors. Traditional Indian coinage was originally based on small rectangular or square ingots of silver or copper and used geometric punch marks whose meaning has been forgotten with the passage of time. Most of these "coins" have multiple punch marks of different types in random patterns. The randomness of these patterns suggests that they may have been added at different times by merchants or government officials as a means of guaranteeing the weight and metallic content of the pieces.

The native Indian tradition was temporarily submerged by Greek concepts of coinage and design in the wake of Alexander the Great's conquest of the northwestern corner of the subcontinent. Under Alexander's Greek and Macedonian successors in Bactria (modern

ABOVE: India, Bactrian Greeks, Apollodotus, Silver Drachm, 160–150 BC
The Bactrian Greeks in India encountered an area that already had a strong, independent coinage tradition—unlike most of the areas that Alexander the Great conquered. The Bactrian Greeks soon created a hybrid coinage, combining Indian and Greek ideas of what money should look like. This coin is based on a Greek weight system, but uses a square design traditional to Indian coinage, and features a bilingual inscription in Greek and Kharoshthi (a language which had its own script).

ABOVE: India, Ghorids of Delhi, Muhammad bin Sam, Gold Tankah, 1205–1206
The Ghorids were an Afghan Islamic dynasty that created the first Islamic empire in India. In 1175 AD, Muhammad bin Sam began the Ghorid invasion that conquered all of northern India. Islamic coinage traditions replaced the indigenous coinage throughout most of India. The result was a new series of coins using old denominations with Arabic script and new designs.

ABOVE: India, Mogul Empire, Akbar, Silver Rupee, 1579
Babar, the great grandson of the Mongol Timur the Lame (Known in the West as Tamerlane) founded the Mogul Empire in 1526 with his conquest of northern India, which united the region under a single empire ruled from Delhi. Akbar, his grandson, created a politically unified empire in which Hindus and Muslims could live together in relative harmony. This lack of civil strife enabled him to rule effectively and expand his domains into the largest empire ever seen in India up to that time. The Moguls were descendents of the Mongol conquerors of Persia, and brought with them the Persian language, which became the standard language for coin inscriptions until the British reform of Indian currency in 1835. First introduced in the tenth century, the rupee increasingly became the standard silver-coin denomination in India.

Afghanistan), northwestern Indian monetary ideas reappeared in the form of square coins with bilingual legends in Greek and Kharoshthi, one of the many languages native to India. These coins spread well beyond the area of their issue and continued to influence money on the subcontinent for many centuries.

Islam began to play an important part in the money of the subcontinent at the end of the twelfth century AD, with the invasion led by Muhammad bin Sam Ghori from Afghanistan. Muhammad took over all of northern India and imposed Islamic principles upon the rule of the region. After his death in 1206, his successors were known as the Sultans of Delhi (the capital of the empire) or the Ghorids, and introduced Islamic coinage practices to India, including identifying the date and place of issue of the coins. For the first time since the Bactrian Greeks, Indian coins could be used as an important source for political history. The successors of the Sultans of Delhi were the Moguls, also from Afghanistan, who took control of northern India under the leadership of Zahiruddin Babar by 1530. In the meantime, Hindu southern India had been united under the Vijayanagar dynasty, which issued only gold coins, known as pagodas.

Europeans began to make an appearance in India after Vasco da Gama's epic voyage around Africa and into the Indian Ocean at the end of the fifteenth century. With the founding of Cochin on the subcontinent's west coast in 1503, the Portuguese began to set up permanent trading stations in India during the early years of the sixteenth century. Several more trading posts were established within a few years, most notably Goa, which remained a Portuguese possession until 1961. These trading posts soon began to issue coins of their own—a precedent that was eventually followed by other European powers in India, including the Dutch, the Danish, the French, and, most importantly, the British. England took a primary role in the money of India from the late eighteenth century onward, as the British East India Company (BEIC) began to nationalize the coinage of the regions under its direct control. By this time, Mogul coinage was being issued by a number of different autonomous principalities throughout northern and central India, without regard to maintaining a single coinage standard—the result was economic chaos, and was the impetus for reforms introduced by the BEIC.

Under English rule, Indian currency was standardized as the silver rupee in 1835, which was adapted from the predominant

ABOVE: India, Orissa, Ganga Kings, Gold Elephant Pagoda, Twelfth Century AD
Pagodas were the standard gold-coin denomination of Hindu southern India for many centuries. From the sixteenth to nineteenth centuries, European colonial powers copied pagodas. The usual designs portrayed various Hindu deities. The Gangas were a group of related princes who controlled much of southeastern India. They were succeeded in southern India by the Vijayanagar dynasty in 1336. The Vijayangars formed a bulwark against the Muslim conquest of southern India for over two hundred years.

ABOVE: India, Portuguese Goa, Manuel I, Gold One-Half Aspera, 1495–1521
The Portuguese were the first Europeans to set up trading posts in India, beginning at Goa on the Indian west coast in 1510. Their trading posts remained active for centuries, in many cases issuing coins for local use well into the twentieth century. Portugal was unusual for a European power in India, because its trading posts never expanded beyond the immediate environs of their original trading stations.

ABOVE: India, British Empire, William IIII, Silver One Rupee, 1835
In 1835, James Prinsep was able to create a new coinage system for the British East India Company's territories. The cornerstone of the new system was a standardized silver rupee designed to replace the over 300 variations then in existence. This new coin greatly facilitated financial transactions throughout India, and was the predecessor of modern Indian coinage.

coinage of northern and central India's then nearly defunct Mogul Empire. This was made possible by the introduction of modern steam-powered coin presses, which incidentally spread the influence of Indian coinage throughout South Asia into Burma, Afghanistan, Pakistan, Bangladesh, the Maldives, and beyond. All of these countries continue to use monetary systems based on the rupee, though with some local alterations.

After World War II, the independence movement in India successfully won the withdrawal of the British in 1947. The Indian Subcontinent then fell into civil war

RIGHT: India, Government of India, Nickel One Rupee, 1950
The newly independent Republic of India issued this coin. The triple-lion statue on the obverse is India's national emblem and is taken from a monumental statue associated with the third-century BC ruler Ashoka. Ashoka was the third king of the Mauryan dynasty who converted to Buddhism and was responsible for its spread throughout much of India. He has become a symbol of Indian independence.

based on religious differences between Hindus and Muslims, which split the former colony into three different countries, based on the predominant religion within each region. India became a predominantly Hindu nation, while Pakistan in the former Northwest Territories, and Bangladesh, in the east, became Islamic nations. The last colonial power to remain on the subcontinent was Portugal, which relinquished its control of Goa to India in 1961. As in other regions of the world, independence resulted in a proliferation of new designs on the money of the region, celebrating the native cultures and history.

India, Mogul Empire, Emperor Jahangir,
Gold Mohur, 1622
In 1618, Jahangir (Akbar's son) introduced a famous series of coins in gold and silver depicting the twelve signs of the zodiac in place of the traditional written month in the dates placed on Islamic coins. These coins are beautifully designed and struck, showing Persian calligraphy at its best, along with interesting and well-executed figures and symbols related to the zodiac corresponding to the month of issue of the coin. This coin depicts Libra, as represented by a set of scales on the reverse, while the obverse gives the date and Jahangir's titles, as well as the mint (Agra).

India, British Empire, Government of India, One Rupee, 1917
This one-rupee note is typical of the types issued by Great Britain for its colonies. In India, the English government was confronted by a colony with a hodgepodge of intermingled ethnic and religious groups, as well as dozens of languages. The note therefore proclaims its denomination in English and eight other languages, each with its own distinct script. Just to make sure, it also has an image of a silver rupee coin of George V, so that there can be no mistake that this note is, indeed, good for one rupee.

ABOVE & DETAIL LEFT: India, Reserve Bank of India, Ten Rupees, 1967–1970
After independence in 1947, India was faced with a problem: how to keep a country with so many distinct nationalities, religions, and languages together. As with the British before them, the Indian government issue money with English, the lingua franca of the country, as the primary language and then include the denomination of the note in fifteen other languages! Hindi is the recognized national language, with 30 percent of the population speaking it. The note features a statue of three conjoined lions—associated with King Ashoka (third century BC) and a symbol of Indian independence.

India, Reserve Bank of India, One Hundred Rupees, 2000

The Indian 100-rupee note features a portrait of Mahatma Gandhi (1869–1948), the
leader of the Indian independence movement and the originator of the concept of
non-violent resistance as a political tool. Gandhi appears on all the denominations
of Indian banknotes, along with a triple-lion statue—both are symbols of Indian
independence. The back of the note has an image of the Himalaya Mountains. As
with earlier notes, the denomination is written out in the fifteen official languages of
India, along with English.

UPPER: India, Reserve Bank of India, 500 Rupees, 2000
The 500-rupee note features Mahatma Gandhi on the front, in common with other Indian banknotes. The back displays a scene of Gandhi leading his followers on the road to freedom.

LOWER: India, Reserve Bank of India, 1000 Rupees, 2000
The 1000-rupee note also features Mahatma Gandhi on the front with the triple-lion statue of Ashoka. The back has a vignette with five scenes showing an allegory of the modern Indian economy—a man on a harvester, a woman at a computer, an offshore oil rig, a satellite, and an automated steel-production plant.

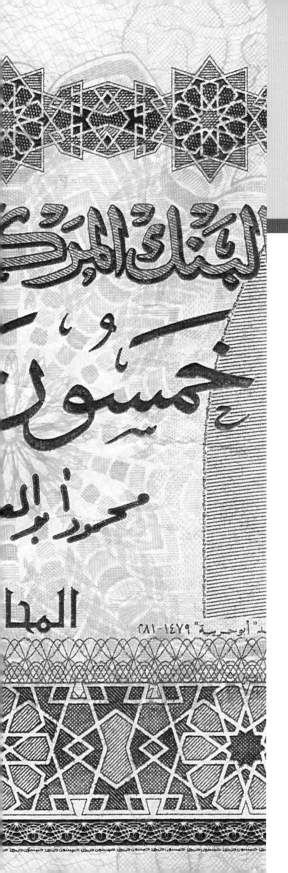

ISLAMIC WORLD

The use of precious metals as money dates back to the ancient civilizations of the Near East. As early as 2000 BC in both Mesopotamia and Egypt, there emerged the practice of carefully weighing pieces of gold and silver to determine their value in paying tribute to local rulers, placing offerings at sacred temples, and performing business transactions. The rise of Islam in the seventh century AD precipitated a fundamental change in the relationship of the Middle East with its neighbors. Islam had its origins in the Arabian Peninsula in the area of Medina, where in 622 AD, a new religion was born. Within one hundred years Islam had spread across all of Arabia and its followers had defeated the Byzantine and Sassanid Persian Empires. After wresting Christian Egypt and Syria from the Byzantines, the Arabs would eventually take all of North Africa before moving on to Spain. However, a reduced Byzantium remained a barrier to further Islamic expansion to the north and west. In the east, the Sassanid Empire, weakened after several decades of warfare with Byzantium, collapsed altogether. By the middle of the eighth century, all of the former Sassanid territories were part of the new Islamic Empire, right up to the borders of India.

DEATIL OF: Egypt, National Bank of Egypt, Fifty Pounds, 2001
The Egyptian fifty pound banknotes feature the Abu Hariba Mosque built by the Mamluk ruler Amir Qijmas al-Ishaqi in 1479-1481.

ABOVE: Umayyad Caliphate, Hisham ibn Abd al Malik, Silver Dirhem, Struck at Wasit, 732 AD
Incorporating the new tenets of Islam within the traditional form of silver coinage, these coins were the direct descendants of the Sassanid drachms. The Arabic legend includes the Shahada (Islamic profession of faith) and passages from the Koran, as well as the place and date of the coins' minting. Wasit is located in present-day Iraq, near Basra. The Umayyad Caliphate had its political capital at Damascus, Syria and was formed in 661 AD.

ABOVE: Samanid Dynasty, Hamid Nuh bin Nasr, Gold Dinar, Struck at Nishapur, 943–954 AD
This coin is an example of the Islamic dinar that replaced the Byzantine solidus as the most important international trade coin during the eighth century. This dinar was produced at Nishapur in Persia by Hamid Nuh I of the Samanid dynasty (819–999 AD). The Samanids were a native Persian dynasty, reflecting the rise of non-Arab groups within the previously Arab dominated Islamic Empire. The Caliphs of the Abbasid dynasty, based in Baghdad, would gradually lose political control of the Islamic Empire while retaining religious authority, much like the Pope in the Roman Catholic Church.

ABOVE: Mongols of Persia, Abu Said, Silver Dirhem, 1322
The Mongols under Genghis Khan began their career of conquest in 1219 AD and soon swept across Asia to the borders of Europe. The string of raids and conquests continued for over one hundred years under the command of Genghis Khan's successors, with catastrophic results for the Islamic world. The Abbasid Caliphate based in Baghdad was destroyed, eliminating the last vestiges of a politically unified Islamic Empire. The Mongol conquest devastated many regions, including Persia, where the Mongol Ilkhanate dynasty was to remain in power from 1256 through 1336. This coin features an ornate Persian form of Arabic script combined with geometric designs.

Islam created a new culture, replacing the old Hellenistic and Persian cultures that had dominated the region for more than 1000 years. This culture was not based on a particular ethnic group or ruling dynasty, but on the concept of a state unified politically by a common religion. The political unity of the Islamic State was to last for well over two centuries and fostered a flowering of art and science and a revival of the knowledge of the ancient world. Islamic invaders entering into Spain from Africa during the early eighth century AD brought this knowledge to Europe. Islamic Spain thus became a center of culture, civilization, and industry through which much of the knowledge of the ancient world was transmitted to the West. Algebra, as well as the use of Arabic numerals and other innovations, also made their way through Islamic Spain to Western Europe.

Surprisingly, the new Islamic State initially had little impact on the coinage of the region. Coins of Byzantine and Sassanid design continued to be used for decades with only slight modification (such as the removal of the cross from Byzantine coins). It was not until the end of the seventh century AD that a distinctive Islamic coinage came into being. This coinage was developed under the Umayyad Caliphate under the Caliph Abd al Malik (691–705). It was characterized by the use of quotations from the Koran as the main design element, along with inscriptions identifying the ruler, mint, and date the coin was made. Over time, the inscriptions became increasingly elaborate, as geometric shapes were added as main elements in coin design. Figural representation disappeared almost completely, replaced by increasingly elaborate forms of calligraphy, particularly in Persia and India.

The standard denominations for traditional Islamic coinages were the dinar in gold (based on the Byzantine gold solidus—the name derives from the old Roman silver denarius); the dirhem in silver (based on the Sassanid silver drachm); and the bronze *fals* (based on the Byzantine bronze follis). Islamic coinage was carried to Africa and Europe, across central Asia to the borders of China, and into India in the wake of conquering armies of the faithful. With few exceptions, the traditional Islamic use of calligraphy and geometric shapes on coinage continued into the

ABOVE: Artuqids of Mardin, Najm ad din Alpi, Bronze Fals, 1152–1176 AD
The Artuqids were Seljuq Turkish mercenaries who gained control of many parts of the Islamic world during the eleventh century. Artuq bin Eseb founded a dynasty in eastern Anatolia that produced a very interesting series of coins based on Greek, Roman, and Byzantine models, despite Islamic restrictions on figural representation. This coin is based on Alexander the Great's portrait found on coins of Lysimachus from the late fourth century BC. Islamic bronze coins were more likely to show figural representations than other types.

ABOVE: Ottoman Empire Mehmet II, Gold Altun, 1478
The Ottoman Turks first made their appearance in history in the thirteenth century under the leadership of Othman, who founded an emirate in Anatolia. By the fifteenth century, the Ottomans had conquered Constantinople and ended the Byzantine Empire, becoming the most powerful state in the Middle East. Eventually, the Ottoman Empire extended from Persia to Hungary and included nearly all of North Africa. The altun was the Ottoman equivalent to the Venetian ducat and became a common trade coin for the Mediterranean region.

twentieth century.

With the end of World War I and the fall of the Ottoman Empire, Westernized forms of currency—introduced by either the English and French colonial authorities or the Republic of Turkey—began to replace traditional Islamic coinage. Figural representations became acceptable on Islamic money for the first time in a millennium, along with the widespread acceptance and use of paper money. By the 1960s, even religiously conservative countries had begun to use paper money and allowed images of political leaders to appear on their currency. This dramatic shift away from traditional Islamic coinage opened the way for a new, diversified means of cultural expression in the twenty-first century. Today, Islamic currency displays a wide range of colors and designs, with themes ranging from secular political imagery to national, cultural, and Islamic religious iconography, reflecting the governments and ethnic heritages of each of the countries.

ABOVE: Turkey, Stainless Steel Two and One-Half Lira, 1975
In 1922 the Turkish Republic under the leadership of Kemal Ataturk replaced the Ottoman Empire. The new Republic was determined to modernize Turkey and create a strong centralized state on the European model. Part of this program included the introduction of new Western-style money. Turkey has since produced an interesting series of coins, such as this one using human figures and Western script—in stark contrast to the strict adherence to Islamic codes of the old Ottoman coinage and that of their neighbors.

ABOVE: Arab Empire, Bronze Follis, Struck at Emessa, ca. 640s AD
The Arabs were relatively slow to create a new coinage in the areas that they conquered, making do with the Byzantine and Sassanid coins already in circulation. Sometimes, the Arabs even used captured dies to strike more. The original designs were eventually altered to reflect the new rulers and propagate Islamic ideals. This coin is an example of a Byzantine design that has been modified by the Arab conquerors.

ABOVE: Algeria, Banque Centrale D'Algerie, Ten Dinars, January 1, 1964
Algeria became an independent country in 1962 after a long, drawn-out war against France. The newly independent country began issuing coins and banknotes soon afterwards in French and Arabic. The front of the note features storks with two minarets in the background. The back displays a scene of women working at traditional crafts.

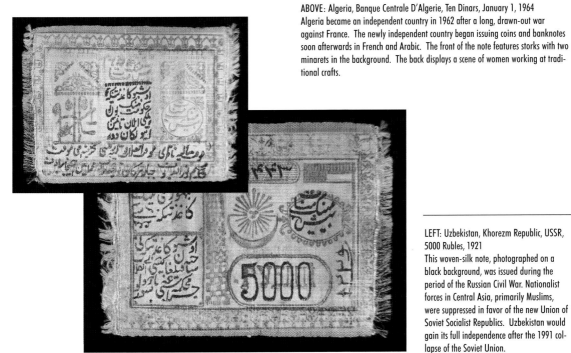

LEFT: Uzbekistan, Khorezm Republic, USSR, 5000 Rubles, 1921
This woven-silk note, photographed on a black background, was issued during the period of the Russian Civil War. Nationalist forces in Central Asia, primarily Muslims, were suppressed in favor of the new Union of Soviet Socialist Republics. Uzbekistan would gain its full independence after the 1991 collapse of the Soviet Union.

Egypt, National Bank of Egypt, One Pound, November 1, 1945
The Egyptian one-pound banknote of 1945 features an image of a young Pharaoh (Tutankamun) on the front. On the back it has an image of a mosque, with the ruins of a small domed building in the foreground. The note was issued during the reign of King Farouk (1920–1965), who ruled Egypt from 1936 until 1952.

UPPER: Egypt, National Bank of Egypt, Twenty Pounds, 2001
The current Egyptian banknote series displays famous mosques on the front and scenes from Egypt's ancient history on the back. The 20-pound banknote features the Mohammed Ali Mosque in Cairo, also known as the Alabaster Mosque, completed in 1857 in the Ottoman architectural style. The mosque is the tomb of Mohammad Ali Pasha (1769–1849), ruler of Egypt under the Ottoman Turks from 1805 to 1848. The back of the note has an image of an ancient Egyptian chariot and scenes from the temple of Sesostris I, Pharaoh from 1971–1926 BC.

LOWER: Egypt, National Bank of Egypt, Fifty Pounds, 2001
The Egyptian 50-pound banknotes feature the Abu Hariba Mosque built by the Mamluk ruler Amir Qijmas al-Ishaqi in 1479–1481. The main element on the back of the note is an interior view of the ancient Edfu Temple, located between Aswan and Luxor and built between 23–57 BC. It is the best-preserved major temple in Egypt. At the top left of the note is a figure of the winged sun with an ancient boat below.

Morocco, National Bank of Morocco, Fifty Dirhams, 1987
Before 2002, all Moroccan banknotes featured a portrait of King Hassan II (1929–1999). Moroccan banknotes issued since 2002
feature a portrait of King Mohammed VI (1963–) on the front, with various buildings in the background. This note features
Hassan II with a fortress in the background. The back of the note displays a scene of the famed Moroccan horsemen charging in
the background, with flowers in the foreground.

UPPER: Morocco, National Bank of Morocco, One Hundred Dirhams, 1987
This Moroccan 100-dirham note has a portrait of Hassan II in front of the minaret of the Koutoubia Mosque in Marrakesh. The back features a painting by Ben Yeseff of a demonstration in favor of the King and several geometric figures.

LOWER: Morocco, National Bank of Morocco, 200 Dirhams, 2002
This 200-dirham note is of the most recent series and features King Mohammed VI with his father in the background and a view of the Hassan II Mosque. The back of the note displays the entrance of the theological schools of the Hassan II Mosque and the top of a minaret, along with various seashells.

1000
BANQUE CEN
000000000
SPECIMEN
No 0050
LE PRESIDENT
LE DIRECTEUR GÉNÉRAL
00000
MILLE FRAN

RALE

SUB-SAHARAN AFRICA

he African continent has been long divided into two major cultural zones by the presence of the Sahara Desert across its northern regions. Africa north of the Sahara has been a crossroad for cultures, as peoples moved between Spain and western North Africa, and from Egypt through Sinai into Asia. As maritime technology developed, cultural contacts were made across the Mediterranean from Europe to Africa and vice versa. The dominant influence in North Africa from the eighth century AD onward has been Islam. In contrast, Sub-Saharan Africa was protected from outside influences by the presence of the vast desert. For thousands of years, explorers could only reach Sub-Saharan Africa by two equally arduous routes: either through the dense jungles of Africa's western coast or by the Nile River. This isolation limited the number of contacts with the outer world and created the impression of mystery that the region retained until the late nineteenth century, which marked the advent of Europeans as explorers and colonizers.

That said, Europeans actually began to explore and establish trading relationships with Sub-Saharan Africans as early as the late fifteenth century. The Portuguese led the way with their attempts to find the sources for West African gold (thus cutting out the Arab middlemen

DETAIL OF: Equatorial African States, Bank of the Equatorial African States, 1000 Francs, 1963
The Bank of the Equatorial African States was the central bank for the group of former French colonies that formed a monetary union in 1961. These countries were the Republic of Congo, Gabon, Central African Republic, Chad, and Cameroon. This note follows the traditional style of French colonial banknotes with lots of color and the use of native imagery. It features a scene of young workers gathering cotton on the front.

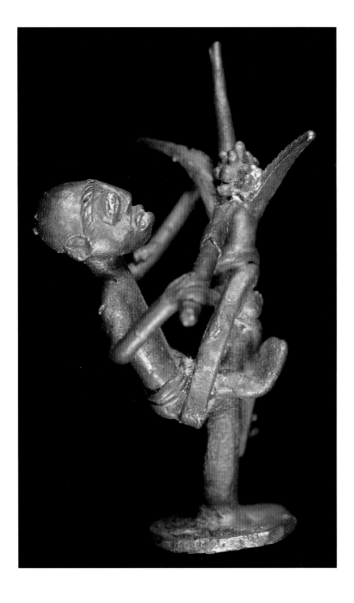

of Morocco and Tunisia) and to discover a direct sea route to India (again to cut out the Arab middlemen—this time of the Middle East). As trade developed with African coastal tribes, European colonial powers needed to develop a mutually accepted means of trading with the peoples of these regions. The Europeans naturally attempted to impose forms of money familiar in Europe, but their efforts met with limited success, due to the strength of traditional cultures and their native forms of money. The result was a dual monetary system, in which European forms of money were used side-by-side with native forms for centuries—particularly in West Africa, where trade contacts were established during the sixteenth century based on the native supplies of gold and the slave trade. Native monies continued to be used in many areas into the mid-twentieth century.

Europeans quickly learned to make use of local currencies, even going so far as to mass-produce certain types of native currency for use in trade; this strategy gave the colonial powers easier access to native economies. The late nineteenth century witnessed the conversion of European coastal trading

ABOVE & OPPOSITE: West Africa, Ashanti, Gold Weights, Nineteenth Century
These statuettes in the shape of a crocodile and a man climbing a tree are brass weights used by the Ashanti peoples of West Africa to measure gold. These objects were produced using an endless array of subjects, including human figures, animals, and ceremonial objects. Although they are not strictly monetary, they are usually included in collections of objects related to the traditional money of Africa.

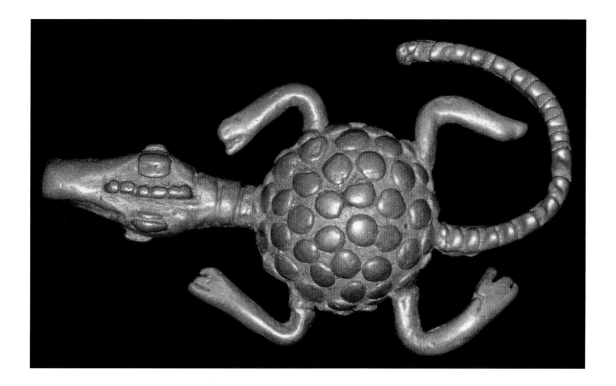

posts—with little or no interest in controlling territories beyond the walls of the posts themselves—to full-fledged colonies, exerting direct political and economic control over the vast majority of the region. By the end of the nineteenth century, only two countries, Liberia and Ethiopia, remained in the control of native rulers.

With the independence of most of the region's countries during the second half of the twentieth century, a plethora of new currencies developed. These currencies reflect the melding of the European monetary tradition with native designs and traditional regional concepts of money. Among

the most beautiful and interesting have been those produced by the former French colonies of Western and Central Africa, which inherited the colorful and artistic French currency tradition. African currency is also notable for its wildlife images, reflecting the natural abundance and diversity of Sub-Saharan Africa's savannas and jungles.

The economic and political turmoil of Sub-Saharan Africa has also resulted in relatively frequent changes in the designs and even in the denominations of money within the region. Close linkages between the French colonies of Western and Central Africa have encouraged the formation

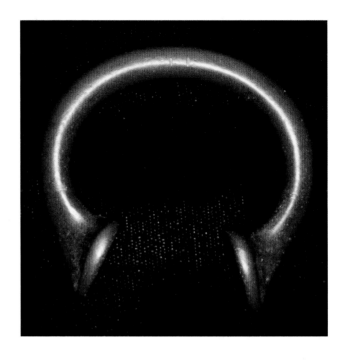

West Africa, Birmingham, England, Bronze Manilla,
Nineteenth Century
Manillas in bronze, copper, or iron were used for centuries in West
Africa, where metal itself was equated with money. The manilla was
convenient to use and was still circulating as late as the 1940s in
some areas. Bride prices and values for slaves were often quoted in
manillas. There were different denominations of manilla, depending
on their size and metal. The largest and rarest was the "King" manilla, worth one-hundred slaves. During the nineteenth century, English
factories in Birmingham produced large numbers of manillas, such as
the example displayed here, for use in the West African trade.

of two separate regional economic and monetary unions since the 1960s. The CFA franc is the common currency of the fourteen former French colonies that comprise the so-called Franc Zone. Benin, Burkina Faso, Côte d'Ivoire, Guinea-Bissau, Mali, Niger, Senegal, and Togo form the West African Economic and Monetary Union (WAEMU), whose common central bank is the Central Bank of West African States (BCEAO). Cameroon, Central African Republic, the Republic of Congo, Gabon, Equatorial Guinea, and Chad form the Central African Economic and Monetary Community (CEMAC), whose common central bank is the Bank of Central African States (BEAC). These organizations have as their goal the abolition of trade barriers among member nations and

the creation of economies of scale through the creation of larger markets—all of which are designed to help spur economic development within the unions. Interestingly, the CFA francs issued by the BCEAO are not legal tender within the CEMAC and vice versa.

The larger and more successful of the two organizations is the West African Economic and Monetary Union (WAEMU), established in 1994. WAEMU has made notable progress developing a competitive common market based on the free flow of persons, goods, services, and capital. CEMAC, also formed in 1994, has been less successful, in part due to the small number of countries involved, their relatively weaker political and economic infrastructure, and also because of a lower commitment level. CEMAC nevertheless plays a vital role in promoting economic cooperation between its member states and fostering the promotion of joint international projects. Both organizations have produced interesting and colorful currency featuring images drawn from their cultural roots and their hopes for economic progress.

South Africa has proven to be the economic power-house of Sub-Saharan Africa, with much of its wealth based on its rich mineral resources. The relative political stability of the country has enabled its economy to continue to grow, despite numerous challenges. These challenges have been reflected on South African money in the shift from imagery celebrating the European heritage of the country, to politically neutral imagery featuring the region's native flora and fauna.

BELOW: Equatorial African States, Bank of the Equatorial African States, 1000 Francs, 1963
The Bank of the Equatorial African States was the central bank for the group of former French colonies that formed a monetary union in 1961. These countries were the Republic of Congo, Gabon, Central African Republic, Chad, and Cameroon. The name of the bank was changed to the Central Bank of the Equatorial African States in 1966, after the five constituent nations entered into a more extensive economic union known as the Central African Customs and Economic Union. With the formation of the Central African States Economic and Monetary Union in 1974, the bank acquired a new name—the Bank of the Central African States. This note follows the traditional style of the French colonial banknotes, with lots of color and the use of native imagery. This note features a scene of young workers gathering cotton on the front and a logging scene on the back—both activities important to the member countries of the monetary union.

1000

BANQUE CENTRALE
DES ÉTATS DE L'AFRIQUE DE L'OUEST

Les auteurs ou complices de
falsification ou de contrefaçon
de billets de banque seront
punis conformément aux lois
et actes en vigueur.

1000 BANQUE CENTRALE 1000
DES ÉTATS DE L'AFRIQUE DE L'OUEST
02144954079

MILLE FRANCS

T   02144954079

LE PRÉSIDENT
DU CONSEIL DES MIN

West African Economic and Monetary Union, Central Bank of West African States, 1000 CFA Francs, January 20, 1992
This note features workmen carrying peanuts at the center, with a woman's head to the right on the front. The back of the note
has an image of two joined statues of a man and a woman and a scene of women carrying baskets in front of elevated storage
sheds built in a lake. The control letter T on the front of the note signifies that this note was issued in Togo.

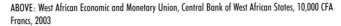
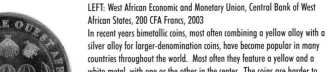

ABOVE: West African Economic and Monetary Union, Central Bank of West African States, 10,000 CFA Francs, 2003

The new 10,000 CFA-franc note features a traditional mask on the front, along with a satellite and an ampersand—all designed to symbolize the West African Economic and Monetary Union's determination to preserve its native culture while moving forward in the modern world. The back of the note displays two colorful Tauraco macrorhynchus birds native to the region of West Africa. This note was issued in Benin, as indicated by the control letter B near the serial number on the front of the note.

LEFT: West African Economic and Monetary Union, Central Bank of West African States, 200 CFA Francs, 2003

In recent years bimetallic coins, most often combining a yellow alloy with a silver alloy for larger-denomination coins, have become popular in many countries throughout the world. Most often they feature a yellow and a white metal, with one or the other in the center. The coins are harder to counterfeit than traditional types and provide an attractive means to easily differentiate denominations. This coin has a yellow-metal center and a white-metal rim and features a traditional mask (also used on banknotes) on the obverse. The reverse features images of staple crops around the denomination of the coin.

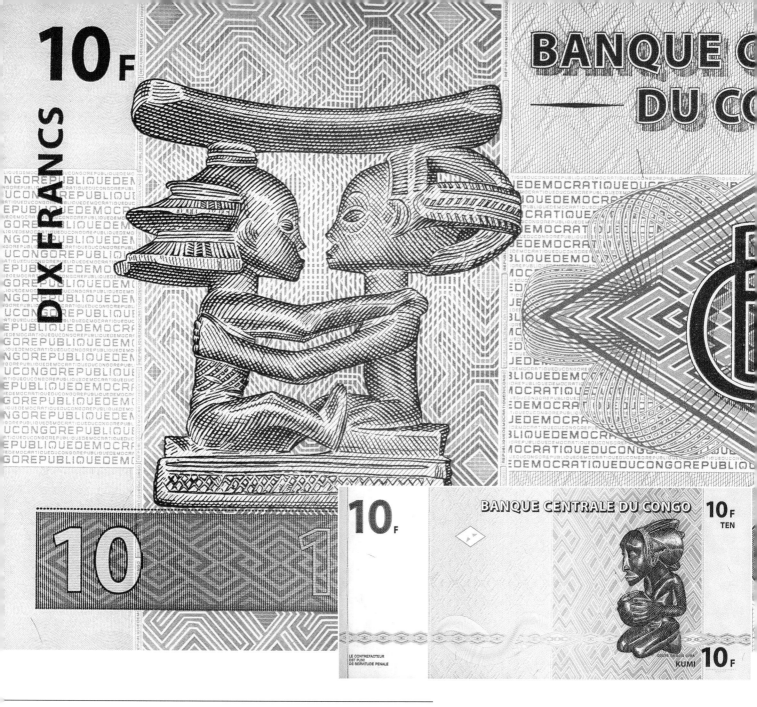

10 F

DIX FRANCS

NGOREPUBLIQUEDEM
UCONGOREPUBLIQU
EPUBLIQUEDEMOCRA
GOREPUBLIQUEDEM
NGORPUBLIQUEDEM
UCONGOREPUBLIQU
EPUBLIQUEDEMOC
GOREPUBLIQUEDE
NGOREPUBLIQUEDE
UCONGOREPUBLIQU
EPUBLIQUEDEMOCRI
GOREPUBLIQUEDEM
NGOREPUBLIQUEDEM
UCONGOREPUBLIQUEP
EPUBLIQUEDEMOCRI
GOREPUBLIQUEDEMO

BANQUE C
DU CO

10

10 F

BANQUE CENTRALE DU CONGO

10 F
TEN

LE CONTREFACTEUR
EST PUNI
DE SERVITUDE PENALE

KUMI **10 F**

Democratic Republic of Congo, Central Bank of Congo, Ten Francs, June 30, 2003
Formerly known as Zaire, the Democratic Republic of Congo was established in 1997 with the fall of
Joseph Mobutu's dictatorial government. The front of the 10-franc note features a carved wooden
headrest. These headrests were used as pillows to preserve the complicated traditional hairstyles.
The back of the note displays another carved statue.

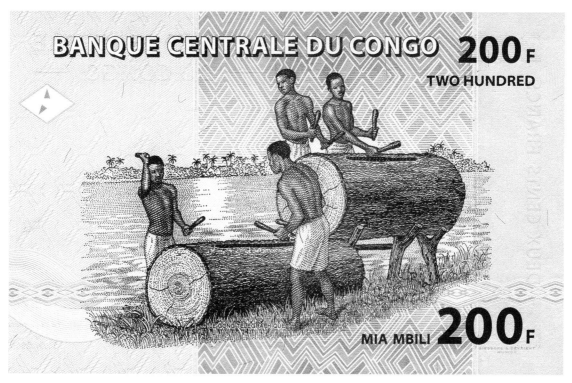

Democratic Republic of Congo, Central Bank of Congo, 200 Francs, June 30, 2003
The front of the Congolese 200-franc note displays a man and a woman working in a field. The back of the note features a group of drummers beating on a drum made from a hollowed-out log.

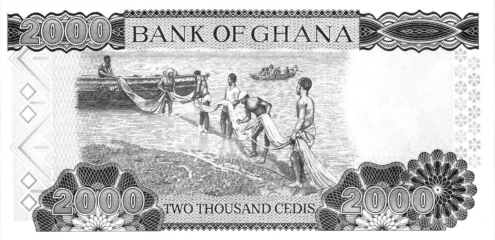

ABOVE: Ghana, Bank of Ghana, 2000 Cedis,
September 2, 2003
The front of the 2000-cedi note features the Ghanaian
coat of arms and a suspension bridge. The back of the
note has a scene of fishermen at work with a net.

Ghana, Bank of Ghana, 5000 Cedis, July 1, 2000
The 5000-cedi note features the Ghanaian coat of arms on the front.
The back of the note displays logs being loaded at the Port of
Takoradi.

ABOVE: Ghana, Bank of Ghana, 500 Cedis, 1996
The obverse of the 500-cedi coin features a set of traditional drums,
while the reverse has an image of the Ghanaian coat of arms.

Ghana, Bank of Ghana, 10,000 Cedis, September 2, 2002
The front of the 10,000-cedi note has a collage of the six leaders of the United Gold Coast Convention (UGCC) who were arrested and detained in 1948 during disturbances in the Gold Coast. They spearheaded the transition of Ghana from colonialism to independence in 1957. They are Dr. Kwame Nkrumah (1909–1972), Dr. Ebenzer Ako-Adjei (1916–2002), Edward Akufo-Addo (1909–1976), Willaim Afori-Atta (1910–1988), Dr. Joseph Boakye Danquah (1895–1965), and Obetsebi Lamptei (1902–1963). The back of the note features the triumphal arch erected in honor of Ghanaian independence.

Ghana, Bank of Ghana, 20,000 Cedis, September 2, 2002
The front of the Ghanaian 20,000-cedi note features Ephraim Amu
(1899–1995), a famous composer and musical performer from Ghana. The
back of the note has an image of a futuristic building, perhaps a concert hall.

SOUTH AFRICAN RESERVE BANK

10

TEN RAND

10

ubowem

Governor

ABOVE: South Africa, South African Reserve Bank, Ten Rand, 1993
Current South African banknotes have an overall theme for their design, an idea common to many countries. The front of the notes features one of the "Big 5" African game animals—the rhinoceros, the elephant, the Cape buffalo, the lion, and the leopard. The back of the notes highlights some aspect of South Africa's economy. The 10-rand note has an image of a rhinoceros on the front. The back features a pastoral scene of a ram's head, with a flock of sheep in the background.

South Africa, South African Reserve Bank, Twenty Rand, 1993
The South African 20-rand note features elephants on the front. The back of the note has a scene of open-pit mining (gold and diamonds are an important part of South Africa's economy), with stylized images of three different styles of diamond jewelry cuts.

LEFT: South Africa, South African Reserve Bank, Nickel-Plated Copper Five Rand, 2002
This coin has the South African coat of arms on the reverse side and an image of a black wilde-beest, or gnu, on the reverse. The coin carries on the South African monetary design theme of including African wildlife on money.

South Africa, South African Reserve Bank, Fifty Rand, 1992
The South African 50-rand note features a male lion's head in the foreground, with two
lionesses and cub drinking at a waterhole in the background. The back of the note shows
the Sasol oil refinery in the background, with a series of atoms in the foreground.

ABOVE: South Africa, South African Reserve Bank,
One Hundred Rand, 1994
This note features a Cape buffalo head in the foreground, with two more
in the background. The back of the note displays a herd of zebras trotting
to the right in the background, with a series of geometric designs in the
foreground.

LEFT: South Africa, South African Reserve Bank, Bronze-Plated Steel Twenty Cents, 2002
The South African 20-cent piece features the flowering protea plant on the obverse, with the
South African coat of arms on the reverse. Coins with steel cores have become common, with
a variety of different alloys used to plate them. Steel is relatively cheap and can be easily
plated, making it a preferred alloy for use in modern coinage.

Tanzania, Bank of Tanzania, 1000 Shilingi, 2000
The older, but still current Tanzanian 1000-shilingi note features the portrait of Julius Nyerere
(1922–1999), a teacher, political activist, and first president of Tanzania (1964) on the front,
along with a vignette of elephants in the lower left. The back of the note has an image of the
Bank of Zanzibar. Zanzibar and Tanganyika joined in 1964 to form the Republic of Tanzania.

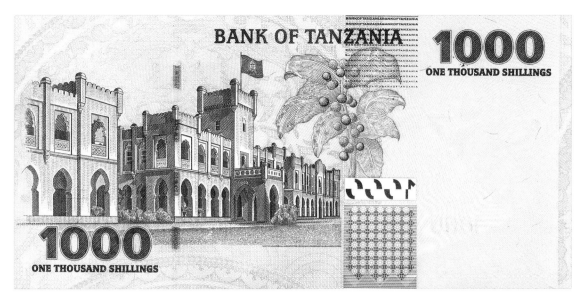

Tanzania, Bank of Tanzania, 1000 Shilingi, February 3, 2003

The new 1000-shilingi note of Tanzania features a similar design to the older note on the front, with the portrait of Joseph Nyerere, but with a scene of rocks instead of elephants. The back of the note features an image of a traditional Zanzibaran-style building. This note is similar to many that have been issued worldwide over the last five years—it has a host of new security features, including security threads, watermarks, fluorescent ink, holographic security stripes, and more.

50 CINC

INSTITUTO

UENTA

SOUTH AMERICA

rancisco Pizarro's conquest of the Inca Empire during the 1530s greatly expanded the Spanish territories in the New World. It also opened up even larger sources of gold and silver than were initially found in the former Aztec Empire of Mexico. The Spanish took full and ruthless advantage of the rich silver deposits in Mexico and South America, particularly the fabled mountain of silver at Potosí, Bolivia. During this time, the earliest coins tended to be crudely struck in order to speed the process of mining, smelting, and accounting the bullion for shipment to Spain. These pieces, known as "cobs," continued to be produced well into the eighteenth century in Lima and certain other Spanish mints. The ad-hoc nature of these early pieces stemmed from the fact that they were only intended to meet temporary local needs. The bulk of the gold and silver was shipped to Spain to be struck into more finished pieces.

ABOVE: Peru, Philip II, Silver Four Reales, 1556–1598
Lima, Peru was made the capital of the Spanish Viceroyalty of Peru in 1542, which consisted of the whole of South America. Peru was split into two new viceroyalties in the eighteenth century—with Lima as the capital of Peru. The major mints of the region were located at Lima and Potosí (now in Bolivia). Lima was chosen as the site for a new mint in 1568. The Lima mint remained active for most of the remainder of the Spanish colonial period and afterwards.

DETAIL OF: Brazil, Banco Central do Brasil, Fifty Cruzados, 1986
The front of this note features a portrait of Oswaldo Cruz (1872–1917), a Brazilian doctor and medical researcher who successfully eradicated yellow fever, the bubonic plague and smallpox as the General Director of Public Health of Rio de Janeiro. The back of the note has an image of the Oswaldo Cruz Institute dedicated to medical research.

BELOW: Peru, Philip V, Gold Eight Escudos, 1715
This coin is an unusually nice example of a cob coin, with clear designs and much of the inscription legible. Cob-type coinages were produced in gold as well as silver, as exemplified by this coin. The basic production method involved casting a crude rectangular bar, which was then hammered roughly into a round shape. The blanks were then cut from the end of the bar, carefully weighed to insure the proper amount of metal, and then struck. The word cob comes from the Spanish "cabo de barra" (end of the bar).

BELOW: Spain, Philip V, Silver Eight Reales, 1630
This coin was struck at the Segovia mint in Spain from silver mined in the New World. It presents a wide contrast with the crude coins produced in the New World at the time—a reflection of the ad-hoc nature of the early minting facilities and the imperative to get silver to Spain as quickly as possible.

After Pizarro's conquest of the Inca Empire, Lima became the capital of the new Spanish Viceroyalty of Peru in 1542, encompassing all of Spain's possessions in South America. Peru was split into two new viceroyalties during the eighteenth century: The northern portion of South America centered on Lima, while the southern portion centered on Buenos Aires. The earliest mints were situated to take advantage of local deposits of silver. Later, new mints were created at provincial capitals to facilitate commerce. The major mints of the Spanish colonial period in South America were located at Lima, Peru (opened in 1568), Potosí (opened in 1575 in what is now Bolivia), and Bogotá, Colombia (opened in 1622).

The colonial coinage of the Spanish New World Empire was struck in standard denominations, of predetermined weight and purity, with uniform designs chosen centrally by royal authorities in Spain. The currency was therefore both remarkably stable and uniform in appearance for over two and a half centuries. The Spanish eight real coin became the world's first truly global coinage, used from the New World to Asia, Africa, Europe, and Australia. Hundreds of millions of these coins were struck during the first two centuries of production alone, making the coinage an essential part of the world economy.

LEFT: Peru, Gold Fifty Soles, 1930
The designs chosen for this coin
highlight the renewed interest of
Latin Americans, and Peruvians in
particular, with their Native
American heritage. The obverse
depicts the head of the last Inca
emperor.

POST-INDEPENDENCE LATIN AMERICA

The wave of revolution that struck Spain's Empire in the New World at the beginning of the nineteenth century eventually led to the formation of a number of independent countries, each of which was eager to establish its own cultural identity. The easiest and most obvious way to proclaim independence was to issue a new coinage—which all of the new countries proceeded to do. In most cases, the standard weight and purity of the traditional eight *real* denomination was retained until late in the century, though the actual names of the coins changed to suit local tastes. Designs were adopted that reflected renewed interest in the native portion of the shared Hispanic and Native American roots of most modern Latin Americans. With the economic upheavals and often-drastic monetary devaluations of the latter part of the twentieth century, many South American countries moved away from a reliance on coinage. Some (such as Bolivia) recently even ceased issuing circulating coins altogether.

Paper money made a late debut in Latin America, in part due to the prevalence of silver, but also because of the region's conservative and slow-growing economy; there simply was not the need for paper currency until the later nineteenth century. Once it did appear, paper money at first followed the pattern and designs of U.S. paper money or that of Great Britain, where most of the money was actually printed. By the early twentieth century, Latin American paper began to reflect the diversity of the native peoples, melded with a strong Iberian overlay. In the 1980s and 1990s, many South American countries began to experiment with new developments that allowed for added security in their paper money, as well as the addition of vibrant colors. This trend has continued to the twenty-first century, with many beautiful currencies reflecting national pride and a rich cultural history being produced throughout the region, often in spite of economic instability and upheaval.

10

DIEZ PESOS

MONUMENTO A LA BANDERA · ROSARIO

MANUEL BEL
(BUENOS AIRES
ABOGADO, P
Y MILITAR, C
DE LA BAN
NACION
EN 181

CASA DE M(

BANCO CENTRAL DE LA
REPUBLICA ARGENTINA   72398105 F

DIEZ PESOS   MANUEL BELGRANO   10

ABOVE: Argentina, Banco Central de la República Argentina, Ten Pesos,
January 14, 1998
This note features the portrait of Manuel Belgrano (1770–1820) on its front.
Belgrano was a statesman and general who led the provinces of Argentina in their
revolt against Spain, beginning in 1810, and created the national flag. The back of
the note has an image of the Monumento a la Bandera (Flag Monument) in
Buenos Aires.

RIGHT: Argentina, General Rosas, Eight Escudos, 1836
This coin is a rare example of the early coinage produced by General Rosas as he consolidated his dictatorship over the
disparate provinces that became Argentina. It has Rosas' bust on the obverse with the legend "Confederated Republic
of Argentina/Rosas." The reverse features a mountain surrounded by water, with crossed canons, muskets, and flags in
the foreground, all surrounded by the legend (translated) "So that the Littoral League Remains Happy," emphasizing
Rosas' primary concern for Buenos Aires, his main power base.

UPPER: Argentina, Banco Central de la República Argentina, Two Pesos, December 1, 1997
The Argentine two-peso note features a portrait of Bartolome Mitre (1821–1906) on the front. Mitre was, a military hero and a journalist, and the President of Argentina from 1862–1868. The back of the notes displays an image of the Mitre Museum in Buenos Aires.

LOWER: Argentina, Banco Central de la República Argentina, Fifty Pesos, July 19, 1999
The front of the Argentine 50-peso note features Domingo Faustino Sarmiento (1811–1888), a famous statesman, educator, and author. As president of Argentina (1868–1874) he was responsible for the expansion of education through building new schools and libraries throughout the country. The back of the note features the Casa de Gobierno (House of Government) in Buenos Aires.

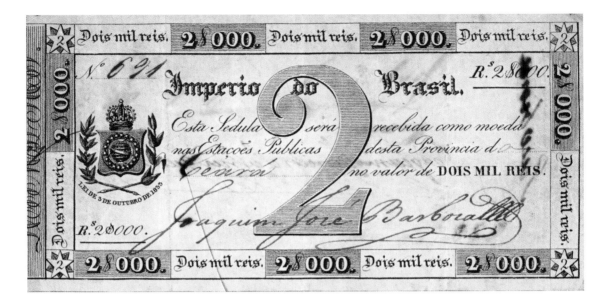

UPPER: Brazil, Brazilian Empire, 2000 Reis, 1833
During the Napoleonic Wars (1799–1815), the Portuguese monarchy transferred the government from Lisbon to Rio de Janeiro in Brazil. After the wars, the Portuguese king returned the government of the Portuguese Empire to Lisbon (1821), but only after an additional five years in Brazil. Brazilian discontent resulted in the establishment of the Brazilian Empire in 1822 under the rule of Pedro, the Portuguese king's son! The Brazilian Empire would last until 1889 and created a period of economic growth and relative political stability.

LOWER: Brazil, Brazilian Empire, 50,000 Reis, 1852–1867
This 50,000-reis note was issued during Brazil's greatest period of economic growth. It reflects the necessary expansion of the money supply through the use of paper money. The note features an allegorical scene of two women on either side of the arms of the Brazilian Empire.

Brazil, Banco Central do Brasil, Fifty Cruzados, 1986
The front of this note features a portrait of Oswaldo Cruz (1872–1917), a Brazilian
doctor and medical researcher who successfully eradicated yellow fever, the bubonic
plague, and smallpox as the General Director of Public Health of Rio de Janeiro. The
back of the note has an image of the Oswaldo Cruz Institute dedicated to medical
research.

Brazil, Banco Central do Brasil, One Real, July 1, 1994
The fronts of Brazilian banknotes of the 1994 series all feature a sculpted head, representing the Brazilian Republic. The different denominations are distinguished by their colors. The backs feature a hummingbird, of which there are more than one hundred species found in Brazil alone.

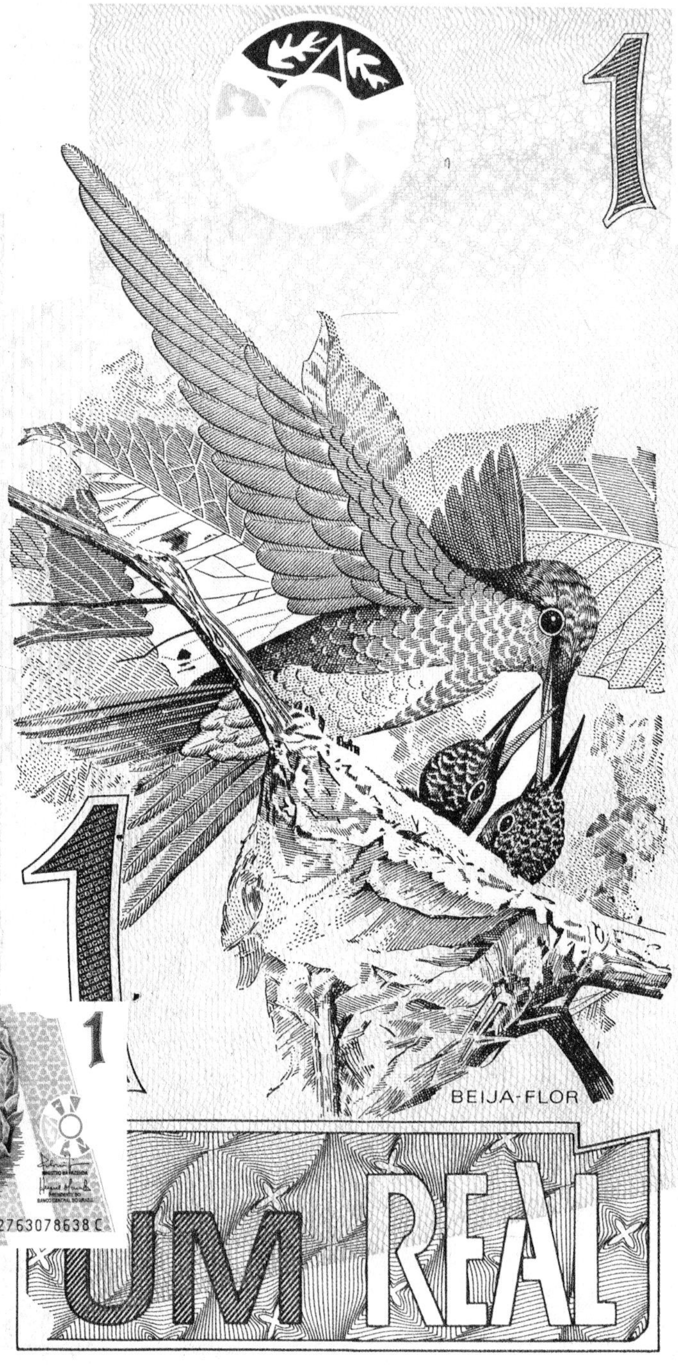
1
BEIJA-FLOR
UM REAL

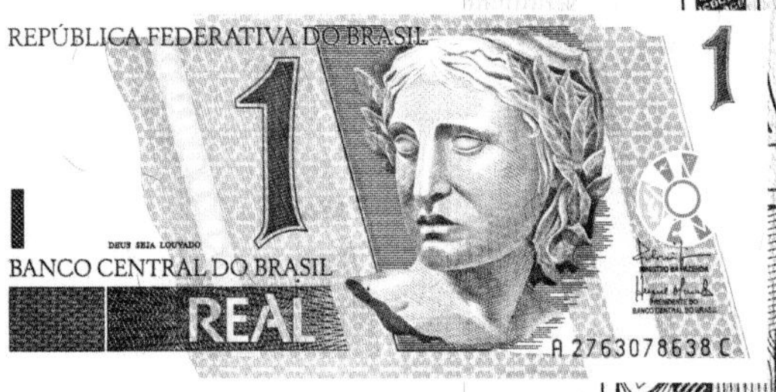
REPÚBLICA FEDERATIVA DO BRASIL
1
DEUS SEJA LOUVADO
BANCO CENTRAL DO BRASIL
REAL
A 2763078638 C

CASA DA MOEDA DO BRASIL

CASA DA MOEDA DO BRASIL

BANCO CENTRAL DO BRASIL

Brazil, Banco Central do Brasil, Five Reais,
July 1, 1994
The front of the Brazilian five-reais note
features a sculptural personification of the
Brazilian Republic. The back of the note
features the great egret, a bird commonly
found in Brazilian wetlands.

Brazil, Banco Central do Brasil, Ten Reais, July 1, 1994
The front of the Brazilian 10-reais note features a sculptural personification of the Brazilian Republic. The back of the note features a greenwing macaw, found in the jungles of South America and one of the largest members of the parrot family.

Brazil, Banco Central do Brasil, Twenty Reais, May of 2002
The front of the Brazilian 20-reais note features a sculptural personification of the Brazilian Republic. The back of the note features a golden-lion tamarind, a type of primate native to the Amazonian jungles and currently endangered in the wild.

Chile, Banco Central de Chile, 10,000 Pesos, 2002
The front of the note has a portrait of Frigate Captain Arturo Prat Chacón (1848–1879), a Chilean naval hero of the War of the Pacific who died fighting against overwhelming odds. The back of the note displays the Hacienda San Agustin de Puñual, birthplace of Captain Prat.

UPPER: Chile, Banco Central de Chile, 1000 Pesos, 2004
The front of the Chilean 1000-peso note features Captain Ignacio Carrera Pinto (1848–1881), a Chilean military hero who died fighting for his country during the War of the Pacific (1879–1884). The back of the note displays the Chilean monument to war heroes, "Chile a sus Héroes."

LOWER: Chile, Banco Central de Chile, 5000 Pesos, 1998
The front of this note has a portrait of Gabriella Mistral (1887–1957), Chilean poet, educator, diplomat, and feminist. Mistral won the Nobel Prize for literature in 1945—the first Latin American woman to do so. The back of the note features an allegorical scene of a muse inspiring a young writer.

Peru, Banco Central de Reserva del Peru, Ten Soles , October 27, 2001
The front of the Peruvian 10-soles note features the portrait of Jose Abelardo Quiñones Gonzalez (1914–1941) and the air-plane in which he was killed. He was a famous Peruvian pilot who became a hero during the border conflict with Ecuador in 1941. The back of the note displays an inverted biplane of the type that Gonzalez flew in air shows during the 1930s.

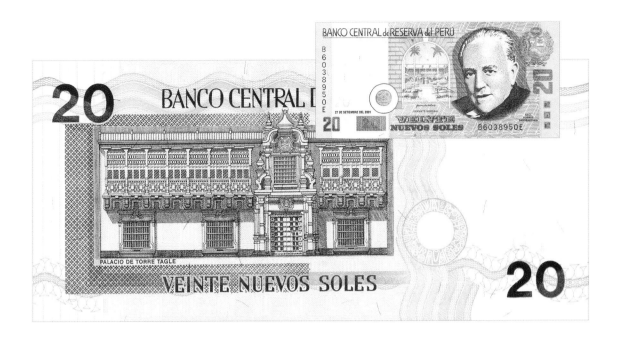

UPPER: Peru, Banco Central de Reserva del Peru, Twenty Soles, October 27, 2001
The front of this note has the portrait of Raul Porras Barrenechea (1897–1960),
historian, diplomat, and university professor. The back of the note features the
façade of the Palacio de Torre Tagle, the Peruvian Chancellery building.

LOWER: Peru, Banco Central de Reserva del Peru, Fifty Soles, October 27, 2001
The front of the 50-soles note displays a portrait of Abraham Valdelomar Pinto
(1888–1919), Peruvian writer, poet, and journalist. The back of the note has an
image of the façade of the Concert Palace in Lima, the meeting place of the
Peruvian intelligentsia of Pinto's time.

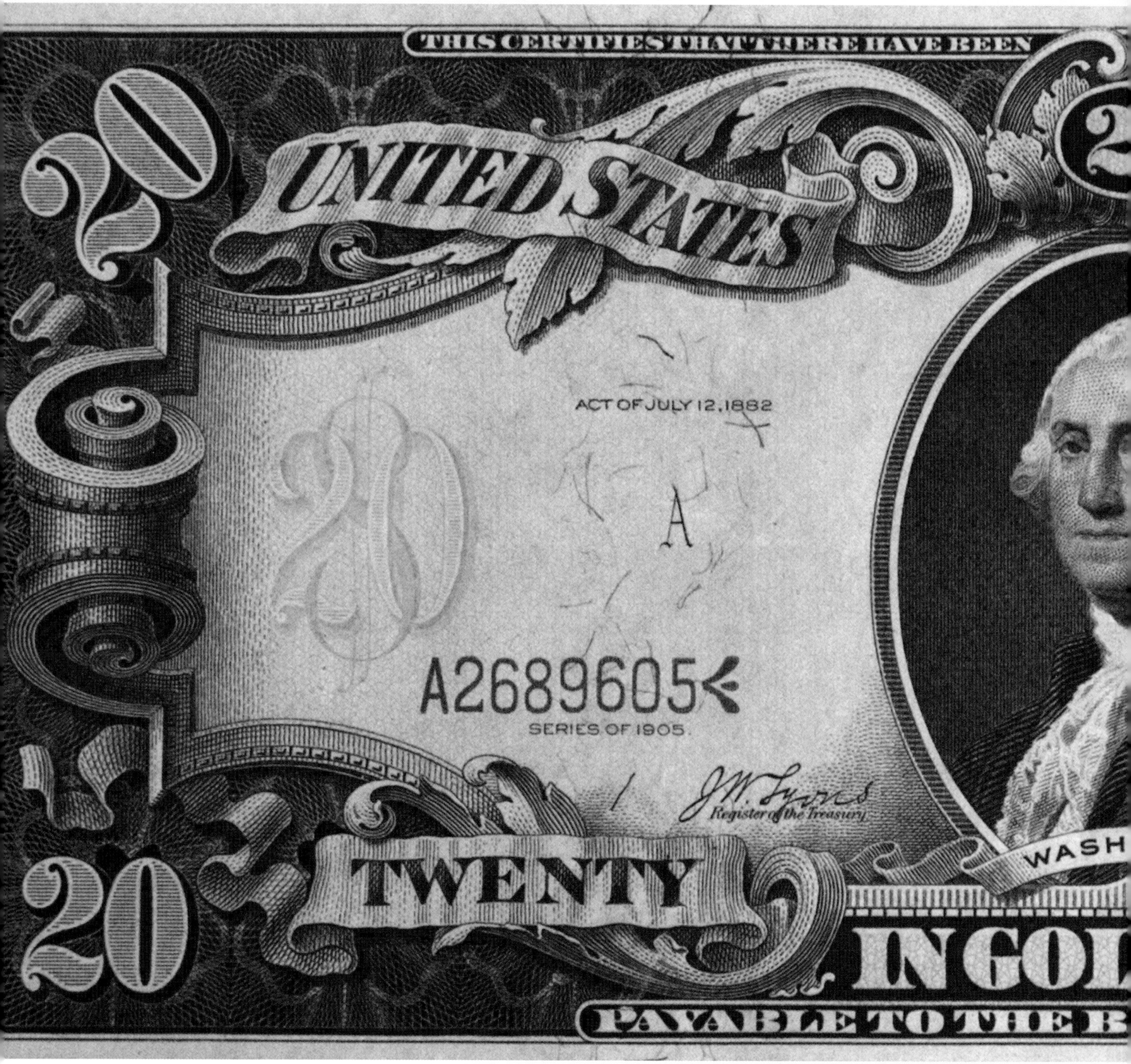

THIS CERTIFIES THAT THERE HAVE BEEN

UNITED STATES

ACT OF JULY 12, 1882

A

A 2689605

SERIES OF 1905.

Register of the Treasury

20

TWENTY

20

WASH

IN GOL

PAYABLE TO THE B

NORTH AMERICA

*T*he settlement of North America began with the Spanish exploration of the Caribbean and its adjoining mainland areas. Mexico became the early jewel in the Spanish crown after its conquest by Hernán Cortés in 1521. Mexico's mineral wealth quickly became legendary and resulted in the early establishment of the first mint in the Western Hemisphere, in 1536 at Mexico City, in order to exploit the major deposits of silver. Mexico would control vast deposits of silver well into the nineteenth century—even after it lost half of its vast northern territory in the Mexican-American War (1846–1848). The Mexican eight *reales*, later renamed the peso, became the dominant silver trade coin of the world, and remained so until the late nineteenth century. This mineral wealth allowed Mexican silver pesos to continue to dominate the international trade market until the end of the nineteenth century—and

ABOVE: Mexico, Charles & Johanna, Silver Four Reales, 1536–1556
This coin is an example of the first series of coins produced in the New World. Mexico City remained a major mint throughout the Spanish colonial period and afterwards. Other early mints included Santo Domingo, Lima, and Potosí. The design of this coin incorporates the Pillars of Hercules (the headland where the Atlantic and the Mediterranean meet), with the legend "Plus Ultra" ("further beyond" in Latin) signifying Spanish claims to the lands beyond the Pillars.

DETAIL OF: United States, Twenty Dollar Gold Coin Note, Series of 1905
Gold Coin Notes were backed by gold coins—you could take one of them in and have it exchanged at any Federal Reserve Bank for U.S. gold coins. This is the famous "technicolor note" named for its multi-color design.

ABOVE & DETAIL: United States, Bank of the United States,
One Thousand-Dollar Interest-Bearing Banknote,
December 15, 1840

This is an interesting example of the obsolete paper money used
in the United States between 1792 and 1866. This was a period
of tremendous economic growth punctuated by severe slumps,
primarily fueled with paper money issued by state-chartered
banks, i.e., up to 8000 individual banks. The ill-fated Bank of
the United States, which fell victim to Jacksonian politics and lost
its position as the central bank of the US, issued this particular
note. It is a genuine example of what is probably the most commonly copied American banknote—the infamous serial number
8894 Bank of the U.S. 1000-dollar note, which has been produced in huge numbers. During the 1960s, a method for producing artificial parchment was developed, which allowed for the
production of "realistic" copies of early US banknotes and
Confederate currency. These notes have been sold as souvenirs or
used in advertising ever since. The Hobby Protection Act of 1973
requires that these reproductions be clearly labeled as copies, but
does not solve the problem of the millions of notes produced
before 1973.

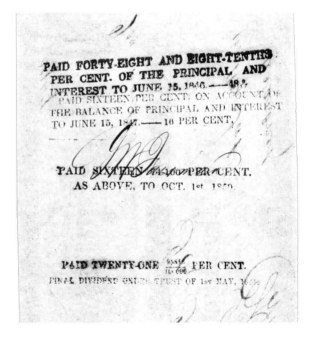

made the development of Mexican paper money largely unnecessary until relatively late. In fact, Mexican bank notes became common only at the very end of the nineteenth century; these early Mexican banknotes followed the conventions of the contemporaneous American banknotes. By the second half of the twentieth century, Mexican money began to undergo a major artistic transformation, which has resulted in the colorful and innovative designs to be found on recent coinage and paper money issues.

Due to the fact that the eastern half of North America was almost totally lacking in deposits of precious metals, colonists in the region, whether French, English, Dutch, Spanish, or Swedish, were forced to develop alternative forms of money. Since only "hard" currency in the form of gold or silver coins was acceptable for international trade, this immediately presented the European colonists with a dilemma—how to get hard money and/or what to use in its place.

United States, Massachusetts Bay Colony, Silver Shilling, 1667–1674
The "Pine Tree shilling" is an early example of the first coinages struck in the English colonies to alleviate the chronic shortage of money. Although they are dated 1652, Massachusetts shillings were struck in several varieties from 1652–1682, with this particular type being struck from 1667–674.

The shortage of silver and gold in North America forced the English and French colonies to be creative in solving their domestic economic needs. Thus fur, nails, tobacco, and just about anything else that could be traded with merchants for European goods were used as money. The search for a stable form of currency eventually resulted in the development of government-backed paper money—the first in the Western world—beginning in the Massachusetts Bay Colony in 1690. Paper money developed into the most common medium of economic growth and a major art form in North America during the nineteenth and early twentieth centuries.

The opening stage of the American Revolution was largely financed through the use of paper money issued by the Continental Congress and the colonial assemblies. Depreciation set in rapidly as the authorities over issued the notes and the British counterfeited them, resulting in a drop in public confidence. By the end of the Revolution, despite the American victory, Continental notes

United States, Continental Dollar, Pewter One Dollar, 1776
This was the first design for dollar coins to be proposed for the United States. These coins were produced in silver, pewter, and brass, and with several minor design variations. Some of these coins circulated but this issue was probably not intended as actual money. These coins have been extensively copied as souvenirs.

were almost worthless, with holders eventually receiving one cent on the dollar more than thirty years after the end of the war. This experience so traumatized the writers of the Constitution that the states were forbidden from issuing money, and the federal government itself refused to issue paper money, except in dire emergencies. The U.S. government would not start issuing paper money on a permanent basis until 1861, as a response to the crisis of the Civil War.

In response to the continued shortage of hard cash in the new United States, state chartered banks began to issue paper money, based on a percentage of their deposits, in order to meet the economic needs of the growing country. From 1790 until 1866, thousands of banks issued paper money, each with their own distinctive designs and denominations, providing a fascinating look into the early history of the country.

ABOVE: United States, Flowing Hair Chain Cent, Copper One Cent, 1793
This coin is one of the finest known examples of the first one-cent coins issued by the Mint at Philadelphia. These early cents are known today generically as large cents, due to their size—it was not until 1857 that the cent assumed its present familiar dimensions at two-thirds the old size.

LEFT: Canada, Colonial Bank of Canada, Five Dollars, May 4, 1859
Banknotes such as this one followed the American model of paper money, issued by state-chartered banks during this time period. The notes were mostly printed by American security printers and used the same styles—and sometimes the same vignettes. The American Banknote Company printed this note in New York.

After World War I, American paper money became the dominant currency of the world, reflecting U.S. economic strength. The Department of the Treasury adapted the designs of American paper money to create a more uniform and easily recognizable appearance. Stability and consistency of design became the guiding principles of American money in order to promote international acceptance and recognition. Coinage too, went into a period of stagnation following an artistic flowering at the beginning of the twentieth century, when major artists, most notably the sculptor Augustus Saint-Gaudens, were commissioned by the U.S. Mint to create outstanding designs for American coins. By the 1940s, American coinage settled into a pattern of uniformity that deadened public interest in coins as collectibles.

United States, Gold Ultra-High Relief Saint-Gaudens Double Eagle, 1907
This coin is considered by many to be the most beautiful piece ever produced by the U.S. Mint. It was designed by the famous sculptor Augustus Saint-Gaudens, in response to a request by President Theodore Roosevelt. Roosevelt was an admirer of ancient Greek coinage and wanted American coins to reflect the same beauty and strength as those of the ancient world. This coin is a pattern piece struck multiple times in order to fully realize Saint-Gaudens' spectacular high-relief design. Only a few of these pieces were struck. Production coins were produced at first with a slightly lower relief for the first part of 1907, but were modified to a new low-relief version by the end of the year, due to technical difficulties at the Mint. It took too many strikes to produce the finished high-relief coins. The new design would continue to be used until the US discontinued the production of gold coins in 1933.

On the eve of the twenty-first century, American money began to change in an exciting and innovative way that promised to end the era of unchanging and dull artistry in the world's most widely used currency. The initiation of the U.S. Mint's Statehood Quarters program in 1999 ushered in an era of artistic innovation in American coins that has raised interest in American coinage to unprecedented levels. At the very end of the twentieth century, American paper money also began to change, this time in response to rampant counterfeiting—and a general desire among certain audiences for a return to more artistically interesting and colorful currency.

United States, Cupro-Nickel Twenty-Five Cents, 2005
In 1999, the U.S. Mint launched a new series of quarter-dollar coins featuring a design on the reverse dedicated to each of the fifty states. The U.S. Mint has released these coins at the rate of five per year, in the order that the states joined the Union. The program has been extremely successful, resulting in a great increase in the number of people collecting U.S. coins. Through their respective images and legends, these quarters provide interesting historical and cultural insights into each of the states.

BELOW: United States, Twenty-Dollar Gold-Coin Note, Series of 1905
Gold coin notes were backed by gold coins—you could take one of them in and have it exchanged at any Federal Reserve Bank for U.S. gold coins. This is the famous "technicolor note," named for its multi-colored design. Recently, the Bureau of Engraving and Printing has gone back to using color on U.S. notes as an anticounterfeiting measure.

BELOW: United States, 500 Dollars FRN, Series 1918
Federal Reserve Notes were created through the Federal Reserve Act of December 23, 1913. These notes were issued in denominations from five dollars to 10,000 dollars. The larger-denomination notes from 500 to 10,000 dollars were first issued as the series of 1918. All of the notes of this first issue feature historical or allegorical scenes on their backs, making them particularly interesting as documents recording America's aspirations and self-image, as expressed by the federal government. The 500-dollar note features a portrait of John Marshall on the front and an engraving of the Spanish explorer Hernando De Soto discovering the Mississippi in 1541.

ABOVE: United States, 100,000-Dollar Gold Certificate, Series of 1934
The 100,000-dollar gold certificate of 1934 was the largest denomination note ever issued by the U.S. government. These notes were produced in the wake of the demonetization of gold in the U.S. in response to the Great Depression. The gold certificates were issued to facilitate balance transfers between the Federal Reserve Banks—they were never circulated in public and ceased to be used after 1946. Note the serial number of this banknote.

ABOVE: United States, Capped Bust Half-Eagle, 1822
This coin is one of three known and is considered to be the most valuable of the U.S. regular issue coins. U.S. gold coins were based on the 10-dollar denomination known as the eagle; the half-eagle was therefore a five-dollar coin. Later, in 1849, a double-eagle would be introduced. This is the heraldic eagle variety of the early gold five-dollar coin. Half-eagles were produced through 1929.

United States, Fifty-Dollar Federal Reserve Note, Series of 2004
The front of the 50-dollar note displays the portrait of Ulysses S. Grant (1822–1885), the eighteenth president of the United States (1869–1877). Grant was the Commander in Chief of the Union Army who had won the Civil War for the Union in 1865, but his administration was best known for corruption despite his personal honesty. The back of the note features the U.S. Capitol in Washington, D.C.

ABOVE: United States, Twenty-Dollar Federal Reserve Note, Series of 2004
The U.S. 20-dollar note has a portrait of Andrew Jackson (1767–1845), seventh president of the United States (1829–1837). He is best known as the winner of the Battle of New Orleans at the end of the War of 1812, and as a "man of the people" who actively sought the popular vote of average Americans. The back of the note features an image of the White House.

BELOW: United States, One Hundred Dollars, Federal Reserve Note, Series of 2001
The U.S. 100-dollar note displays the portrait of Benjamin Franklin (1706–1790), one of the most famous and beloved of Americans. He was a printer, scientist, inventor, economist, statesman, philosopher, musician, and Founding Father of the United States. The back of the note features an image of Independence Hall in Philadelphia.

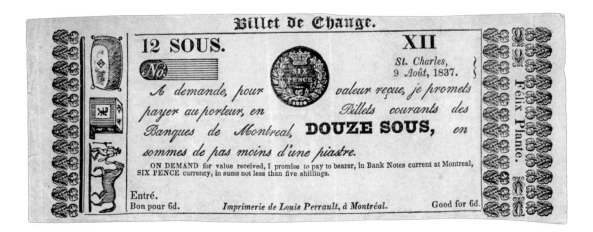

UPPER: Canada, Louis Perault,
Twelve Sous/Sixpence, 1837
This note was issued in Montreal,
Quebec, Canada, in both French and
English. Interestingly, it also uses
two different but equivalent denominations—one for those familiar with
French currency denominations, and
one for those familiar with English
denominations. Merchant notes such
as this formed the backbone of local
small trade throughout much of the
nineteenth century in Canada.

LOWER: Canada, Dominion of Canada, Twenty-Five Cents, July 2, 1923
Before the Bank of Canada began to issue the exclusive legal tender paper
currency for Canada in 1935, private banks followed the Canadian govern-
ment-issued banknotes. This banknote, issued by the Dominion of Canada, is
known as a "fractional" note because it has a denomination of less than one
dollar. Fractional notes normally signify a shortage of the equivalent
coinage, either due to the inability of the mint to produce a sufficient quanti-
ty, or because of economic difficulties, such as a depression or recession.
During such economic crises, people tended to hoard coinage, because of the
intrinsic value of its metal, i.e., silver or gold.

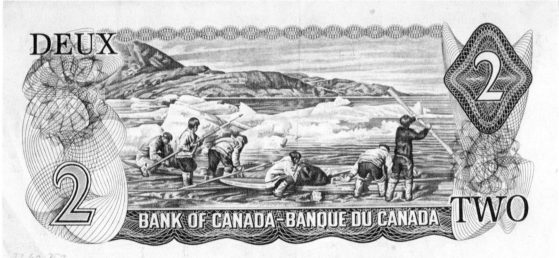

Canada, Bank of Canada, Five Dollars, 1972
The Bank of Canada began issuing Canadian paper money in 1935. Since that time, Canadian paper money has been issued in six different series. This note belongs to the series of 1969–1979, which introduced the use of color-shifting pigments below the dominant color. This note has the portrait of Sir Wilfred Laurier (1848–1919), the first French-Canadian Prime Minister of Canada (1896–1911). The back of the note features a salmon boat fishing off the coast of Vancouver, British Columbia.

Canada, Bank of Canada/Banque du Canada, Ten Dollars, 2005

Sir John A. Macdonald (1815–1891), Canada's first prime minister and one of the Fathers of Confederation, is featured on the front of the 10-dollar banknote. Macdonald was Prime Minister from 1867 to 1873 and from 1878 to 1891. He is remembered as a nation builder—and for building Canada's transcontinental railway. The back of the note commemorates remembrance and peacekeeping, with an image of a veteran and two young people observing a Remembrance Day service (Remembrance Day commemorates the end of WWI) as members of the Land and Naval Forces stand vigil. The first verse of John McCrae's poem, *In Flanders Fields*, and its French adaptation, *Au Champ d'Honneur*, by Jean Pariseau, are featured together with doves and a wreath of poppies.

Canada, Bank of Canada/Banque du Canada, Twenty Dollars, 2004
The 20-dollar note has a portrait of Queen Elizabeth II. Canada is a constitutional monarchy and a member of the British Commonwealth, with Queen Elizabeth II as the reigning monarch and head of state. Depicted on the back of the note are The Spirit of Haida Gwaii, The Raven and the First Men, The Grizzly Bear, and Mythic Messengers by Canadian artist Bill Reid. Reid was an influential artist whose work continues to inspire Canadian artists. The accompanying quote is an excerpt from Gabrielle Roy's novel, *The Hidden Mountain*, about the influence of arts and culture in defining a society.

Canada, Bank of Canada/Banque du Canada, Fifty Dollars, 2004
The 50-dollar note features a portrait of William Lyon Mackenzie King, Canada's longest-serving Prime Minister (1921–1930 and then 1935–1948). King was responsible for important social reforms for unemployed workers and for families. The back of the note celebrates Canadian nation-building with images of the Thérèse Casgrain Volunteer Award medal and scenes from Canadian legal history. The quotation reads "All human beings are born free and equal in dignity and rights" and is from the Universal Declaration of Human Rights.

Canada, Bank of Canada/Banque du Canada, One Hundred Dollars, 2004
Sir Robert Laird Borden, Canada's Prime Minister from 1911 to 1920, is featured on the front of this note. Borden led Canada during World War I and was instrumental in promoting Canadian interests during the negotiations that ended it. The back features a map of Canada created by Samuel de Champlain in 1632, a birch bark canoe, a satellite image of the country, and a satellite, all celebrating Canada's achievements in exploration. It also includes an excerpt from Miriam Waddington's poem, *Jacques Cartier in Toronto,* in French and English.

Mexico, Banco de México, Twenty Pesos, April 17, 2001
The front of this note features the portrait of Benito Juárez
(1806–1872). Juárez was a Zapotec indian who served two
terms (1861–1863 and 1867–1872) as president of Mexico.
Juárez is often regarded as Mexico's greatest and most beloved
leader. He was the only Native American to serve as Mexico's
President. The back of the note shows the Ampitheatre of
Juárez, a monument erected in Benito Juárez's memory.

UPPER: Mexico, Banco de México, Fifty Pesos, March 17, 1998
The front of this note displays a portrait of Jose Maria Morelos (1765–1815), the Mexican patriot who, along with Miguel Hidalgo, began the Mexican Revolution against Spain. The back of the note features a scene of fishermen off of the coast of the Mexican state of Michoacan.

LOWER: Mexico, Banco de México, One Hundred Peso , April 23, 2003
The front of the 100-peso note features a portrait of the Inca Emperor Nezahualcoyotl. The back of the note has an image of Xochipili, the Aztec god of love, games, beauty, dance, flowers, maize, and song.

Mexico, Banco de México, 200 Pesos, October 18, 2000
The front of this note features a portrait of the nun/writer Juana Inés
de la Cruz (1648–1695), with books in the background. The back of
the note displays an image of the Convent of San Jeronimo.

UPPER: Mexico, Banco de México, 500 Pesos, October 18, 2000
The front of the Mexican 500-peso note features a portrait of General Ignacio Zaragoza (1829–1862), victor of the Battle of Puebla, with a battle scene in the background. The back of the note has an image of the cupola of the Cathedral of Puebla.

LOWER: Mexico, Banco de México, 1000 Pesos, March 26, 2002
These notes feature a portrait of Miguel Hidalgo y Costilla (1753–1811), the Catholic priest who is credited with beginning the Mexican War of Independence against Spain. The reverse of the note depicts the University of Guanajuato, founded in 1732 and one of the oldest and best universities of Mexico.

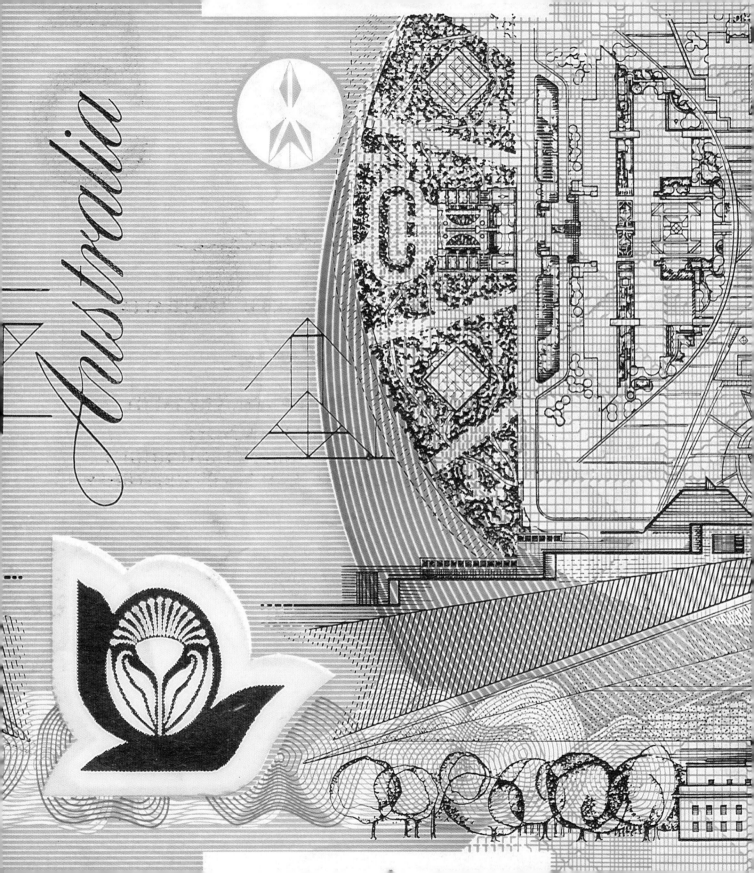
Australia

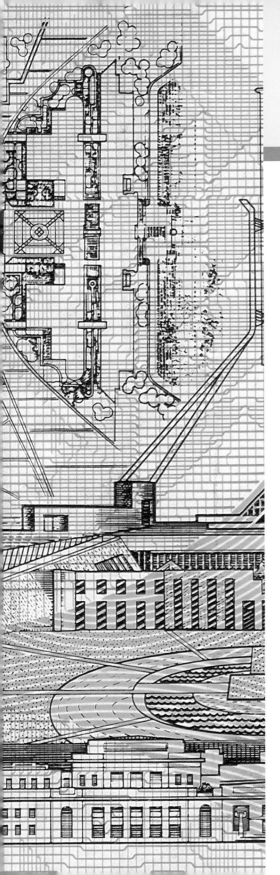

AUSTRALIA AND OCEANIA

Oceania consists of the island nations of the Pacific Ocean and its peripheries, including Australia and New Zealand. The region was settled by several distinct groups of people. Polynesians and Melanesians of Southeast Asia came via ocean-going canoe to the region, which they've occupied over the last 4000 years. And approximately 40,000 years ago, Australian Aboriginals crossed a land bridge formed during the last glacial period to settle in Australia and its nearby islands. All of the indigenous peoples of Oceania formed largely insular societies with relatively few contacts with the outside world, due to the huge transoceanic distances involved. This region was largely unaffected by the outside world until the late eighteenth century, when Europeans began colonizing the various islands, including the continent of Australia. The money of Oceania, to the extent it was used, was based on various natural products such as animal teeth, rock, shells, and feathers. The value of these traditional monies was often based on the difficulty of obtaining or producing them. For example, sperm-whale teeth were

LEFT: Fiji, Whale-Tooth Money, Nineteenth century
On the island of Fiji, larger transactions generally involved the payment of a whale's tooth. A single tooth could purchase a seagoing canoe. During some periods, the teeth were so valuable that only chiefs could hope to own them. Their value was based on the difficulty of hunting and killing the sperm whale, the source of this specimen.

DETAIL OF: Australia, Reserve Bank of Australia, Five Dollars, April 24, 1995
This polymer note design was first issued in 1995. It features a portrait of Queen Elizabeth II on the front with a clear plastic "window" incorporating a gumflower. The back of the note features interesting plan views of the Australian Parliament house.

Hawaii, King Kamehameha III, Copper One Cent, 1847
King Kamehameha I (ca.1758–1819) united the islands of Hawaii into one kingdom during the first decade of the nineteenth century. This kingdom was to last
until 1893, at which point Queen Liliuokalani (1838–1917) was deposed and a
pro-American provisional government installed. Hawaiian coinage began in
1847 with the production of a one-cent piece. King Kalakaua (1836–1891) produced the first comprehensive coinage in 1883 based on the silver dala (dollar).

used as currency in Fiji. Natives of the Yap Islands (Micronesia) used their famous stone money, which had to be transported hundreds of miles across the ocean in open canoes from the island of Palau.

During the early eighteenth century, the increasingly frequent visits by European and American sailors to the islands of the Pacific began to include settlers, traders, and missionaries, who wanted to create a permanent presence in the region. As a result, European concepts of money began to appear. The strong centralized king-dom of Hawaii, united for the first time under the rule of King Kamehameha I, "the Great," in 1810, produced the first modern native coinage of the region during the 1840s. In 1847, King Kamehameha III issued the first Hawaiian coinage, modeled after the coins of the United States, an increasingly strong presence on the islands, both culturally and economically. Over the remainder of the century, Hawaiian coinage expanded as trade relations with the outside world, particularly the United States, became stronger.

As Europeans and their influence became more common, European-style money came into use, at first in the form of the common world trade coins of the time, in particular the Spanish silver dollar (or eight *real* coin), Dutch guilders, English shillings, and Portuguese or Indian gold coins. The earliest coinage in the region was produced in the early nineteenth century at New South Wales in Australia, where the authorities punched holes out of Spanish dollars. The resulting cutout and the host coin were then countermarked with their new values and used as separate coins. After the discovery of gold in Australia, mints were set up at several locations to produce gold sovereigns of British pattern. These sovereigns became the first distinctive official currency produced for the continent for regular use.

European-style coinage was not common in Oceania, with the exception of Australia, New Zealand, and Hawaii, until the beginning of the twentieth century, when European colonial powers began to issue currency specifically for use in their possessions. These coinages and paper money reflected the tropical beauty and cul-

Australia, Queen Victoria, Gold Sovereign, 1855
After the discovery of gold in Australia in 1850, several mints were established in the colony in order to process the gold and produce coinage. This coinage was declared legal tender throughout the British Empire in 1866; in 1877 the design was changed to match that of the imperial sovereigns, with the exception of a mintmark. This piece was struck at the mint in Sydney, which began operations in 1854.

157

tural diversity of the region, combined with European imagery implying the beneficial effects of European rule. As the island nations became independent in the wake of World War II, new money was produced reflecting a more purely native viewpoint.

As the economic powerhouses of the region, Australia and New Zealand have led the way in the introduction of new and interesting money, particularly paper currency. These notes reflect the rich and varied cultural inheritance of the two nations, from the English and Scottish settlers to the Australian Aboriginals and the New Zealand Maoris. The result has been colorful, visually interesting, and culturally informative money reflective of the values of their people. Leading the way in the production of colorful and innovative banknote designs, Australia introduced the first successful polymer (a form of plastic) banknotes in 1988. Since that time, twenty-six countries, including several countries in Oceania (whose money is produced in Australia), Malaysia and Mexico, have started using polymer for all or some of their banknotes.

Fiji, Queen Elizabeth II, Cupro-Nickel Sixpence 1953
Fiji was among the first of the Pacific island countries to have its own coinage, starting in 1934. Fiji remained a part of the British Commonwealth until 1970, and thus displays Queen Elizabeth II on its coinage as its head of state. The Royal Mint in London struck these coins.

ABOVE: French Pacific Territories, 500 Francs, 1992
The French territories in Polynesia are governed from the capital of Papeete in Tahiti. This note features Tahitian natives and island scenes, along with outrigger canoes and Tahitian traditional wood carvings.

LEFT: French Pacific Territories, Aluminum Five Francs, 1952
The French territories of the Pacific Ocean share a common currency—the French franc. The notes and coins issued for the region feature scenes drawn from the various islands, combined with images of France as a benign protector. The obverse of this coin has an allegorical image of France holding the torch of knowledge and a cornucopia (signifying plenty). The reverse of the piece has an image of outrigger canoes, with palm trees and an island in the background.

Fiji, Reserve Bank of Fiji, One Dollar, 1987
Modern Fijian currency retains the portrait of Queen Elizabeth II as the head of state. Fiji became
independent from the United Kingdom in 1970; its currency board became the Reserve Bank of
Fiji in 1984. This note features Queen Elizabeth II's portrait on the front with the coat of arms of
Fiji. The back of the note has a scene of a Suva market, with a cruise ship in the background.
Both sides display an intricate series of geometric designs with a Fijian theme.

Fiji, Reserve Bank of Fiji, Five Dollars, 2002
This five-dollar note of Fiji displays Queen Elizabeth II on the front with the coat of arms of Fiji, a small bird (a "bunedamu") and an ornamental canoe prow (the symbol of the Reserve Bank of Fiji that appears on all Fijian banknotes). The back of the note features Nadi International Airport, with an inset of a Bimaran tour boat.

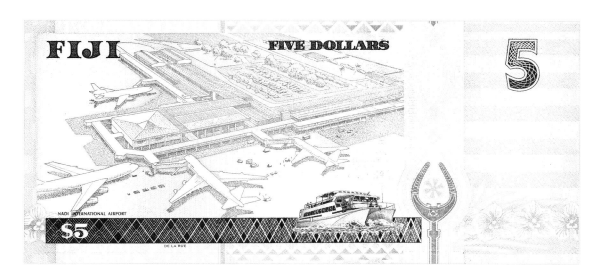

ABOVE: Australia, Commonwealth of Australia, One Pound, 1913–1918
This note was issued after the formation of the Commonwealth of Australia, which united the previously separate colonies of the continent. The note follows the typical pattern of paper money issued throughout the British Empire at the time.

BELOW: Australia, Reserve Bank of Australia, Five Dollars, April 24, 1995
This polymer note design was first issued in 1995. It features a portrait of Queen Elizabeth II on the front, with a clear plastic "window" incorporating a gumflower. The back of the note features interesting plan views of the Australian Parliament house.

Australia, Reserve Bank of Australia, Ten Dollars, November 1, 1993

This polymer note design was introduced in 1993. On the face side, the note features A.B. Paterson (1864–1941), better known as "Banjo" Paterson. Paterson was an Australian poet best known for writing the lyrics to the internationally known folk song *Waltzing Matilda,* which many Australians regard as their national anthem. The back of the note has a portrait of Dame Mary Gilmore (1865–1962), a famous Australian poet and activist who worked for women's rights and to improve the treatment of Australian Aboriginals. The note includes a clear plastic window incorporating a windmill.

Australia, Reserve Bank of Australia, Twenty Dollars, October 31, 1994

Introduced in 1994, the Australian 20-dollar note features a portrait of Mary Reibey (1777–1855), an early Australian convict-turned-entrepreneur who managed to become a successful businesswoman after enduring many hardships. The back of the note honors John Flynn (1880–1951), a minister who became a driving force behind the opening up of the Australian Outback through the establishment of better communications, and the Royal Flying Doctor Service, which provides medical service to the isolated residents of the region. The plastic window on this note features a compass.

UPPER: Australia, Reserve Bank of Australia, Fifty Dollars, November 4, 1995
The Australian 50-dollar note, introduced in 1995, features the portrait of David Unaipon (1872–1967), the first published Aboriginal author. Unaipon was an inventor and an activist for Aboriginal rights. The back of the note has a portrait of Edith Cowan (1861–1932), the first woman to be elected to an Australian Parliament. Cowan was also a noted activist for women and children, and a member of the bench of the children's courts. The plastic window on this note features the stars of the Southern Cross.

LOWER: Australia, Reserve Bank of Australia, One Hundred Dollars, May 15, 1996
This note features on its face the portrait of Australia's famous soprano, Helen Porter Mitchell (1861–1931), known as Dame Nellie Melba. Melba was considered the best soprano in the world of her time. The back of the note features John Monash (1865–1931), the most famous Australian general of World War I, and a noted engineer and educator. The plastic window displays an image of a lyrebird.

New Zealand, Reserve Bank of New Zealand, Five Dollars, October 18, 1999

The New Zealand five-dollar note is a polymer note that features Sir Edmund Hillary (1919-), the country's famous explorer. Hillary was the first man to climb Mt. Everest (1953), and the first to drive overland to the South Pole (1958). The note also displays Mt. Cook, the highest of New Zealand's mountains, and the tractor used in Hillary's drive to the South Pole. The back of the note highlights Campbell Island, the yellow-eyed penguin (or "hoiho," in Maori), and diverse flora native to the island. The note has two plastic windows.

UPPER: New Zealand, Reserve Bank of New Zealand, Ten Dollars, May 10, 1993
This 10-dollar note is an older paper note that was replaced in 1999 by a polymer note of similar design. It features Kate Sheppard (1847–1934), the noted New Zealand activist for women's suffrage. Her leadership resulted in New Zealand becoming the first country in the world to extend voting rights to women in 1893. The white camellias depicted are associated with Sheppard's suffrage movement. The back of the note displays the endangered blue duck ("whio" in Maori).

LOWER: New Zealand, Reserve Bank of New Zealand, One Hundred Dollars, July 26, 1999
First issued in polymer in 1999, the New Zealand 100-dollar note features Lord Ernest Rutherford (1871–1937) on the front, along with the an image of the Nobel Prize medal he won for chemistry in 1908 for his research on atoms. The back of the note displays a yellowhead, or bush canary, and flora found on New Zealand's South Island. The note has two plastic windows.

50

iBhanki enguVimb

Bannga ya Vhukati y

APPENDICES

- NUMISMATIC GLOSSARY

- COLLECTING COINS AND CURRENCY

- NUMISMATIC BIBLIOGRAPHY

DETAIL OF: South Africa, South African Reserve Bank, Fifty Rand, 1992
The South African 50-rand note features a male lion's head in the foreground, with two
lionesses and cub drinking at a waterhole in the background. The back of the note shows
the Sasol oil refinery in the background, with a series of atoms in the foreground.

Numismatic Glossary

Anepigraphic: No inscription.

Attribution: Interpreting and recording the details of a coin's legends and symbols.

Back: Used to identify the backside of a banknote; opposite of front.

Billon: Silver colored base metal.

Bimetallic: 1) A coinage issued in two metals, as in gold and silver coins. 2) Modern coins incorporating two different color metals.

Bourse: The sales floor of a coin show or convention.

Bracteate: Thin coin, struck only on one face.

Brockage: Mis-struck coin; same design on both sides, one incuse.

Bust: Portrait of a person that includes the shoulders.

Celator: Artist who carves the dies for striking coins.

Contorniate: Large Roman coin-like medallion.

Countermark: Small punch mark added to a coin-often used by a mint to reissue a coin at a different value.

Denomination: Assigned value of a coin or paper money.

Die: Engraved metal cylinder used to transfer an image to a coin.

Die-axis: Relative position of the obverse vs. the reverse designs on a coin expressed in degrees, using a 360 degree circle.

Die link: Two coins whose obverses or reverses share a common die.

Double strike: Coin error caused by repetitive striking of a planchet.

Electrum: Naturally occurring alloy of gold and silver.

Exergue: Small space at the bottom of a coin's design.

Field: Flat space around a main design of a coin.

Flan: Blank piece of metal used to produce a coin.

Fleur de Coin: FDC, the flower of coinage, mint condition.

Fourré: Plated coin with a copper or lead core.

Front: The front of a banknote; opposite of back.

Hammered: Struck by hand with a hammer.

Head: Portrait of a person without the shoulders.

Hoard: Group of coins found together, usually buried for safe-keeping.

Incuse: Design that is recessed into the surface of a coin.

Inscription: The words on a coin-also known as the legend.

Intaglio: Engraved into the surface in negative-as in a coin die.

Legend: Words on a coin - see inscription.

Mint: Where coins are made.

Mint-mark: Symbol, letters or monogram indicating where a coin was struck.

Module: Size of a coin expressed as the diameter and sometimes the thickness.

Moneyer: Individual responsible for striking an issue of coins.

Mule: Coin created from the striking of two normally unrelated dies.

Obverse: 'Heads' side of a coin, opposite of reverse.

Orichalcum: Brass alloy-most often associated with ancient Roman coins.

Patina: Oxidation on a coin's surface.

Planchet: Flat metal disk ready to be made into a coin.

Retrograde: Inscription in which the letters run opposite to the norm (i.e., right to left instead of left to right).

Reverse: "Tail" side of a coin; opposite of obverse.

Scyphate: A coin that is concave.

Stater: A standard unit of weight-often used as the main denomination of Greek coins.

Type: Main features of a coin's design that distinguishes it from others.

Uniface: Coin struck only on one side.

Verdigris: Green crust of copper sulfate or copper chloride on a coin's surface.

Watermark: Design produced on paper that can only be seen when raised to a light. Used as a security device on many modern banknotes.

COLLECTING COINS AND CURRENCY

CHOOSING A THEME

The first thing to do is to think about what you want to collect. What are you interested in? Do you enjoy coins, or is paper money more interesting to you? What can you afford? There is nothing so frustrating as finding out that the collection you have started is too expensive for you to keep up.

There are lots of possible themes to use in collecting—choose one that is exciting for you and stick to it. Here are some ideas:

- Collecting by state—the new statehood quarters are popular and easy to collect. You can also make interesting collections of commemorative coins or the U.S. National Bank note series.
- Collecting a set of world coins by country—many people try to get an example of a coin from every country in the world.
- Collecting by year—other people collect coins struck in the year they were born, or from some other date of importance to them.
- Collecting by denomination—this is a collection that, for example, could include all the different types of dimes produced by the U.S. Mint.
- Collecting by design—some collectors base their collecting on images of ships on coins or on paper money, or elephants, eagles, etc. This type of collecting is interesting because it can include money from all over the world, and both modern and ancient coins.

Once you have a theme, you will want to learn as much as you can about it.

Learning More

First, find a reference work that covers your collecting interest.

- For U.S. coins, *A Guide Book to United States Coins* by R. S. Yeoman is an excellent beginning reference.
- A good guide for U.S. paper money is Gene Hessler's *The Comprehensive Catalog of U.S. Paper Money*.
- For world money, there is Krause and Mishler's *Standard Catalog of World Coins* and the companion *Standard Catalog of World Paper Money*.

Of course, the Web is also a great place to look for information on coins and paper money. Your local museum may even have a numismatics collection. Remember, the more you know, the easier it will be to start collecting.

Beginning to Collect

It's easy to start a coin collection. You can start at home by collecting coins that you have around your house. Ask friends and family for help. Ask if they have any interesting coins from faraway places. They can also help you look for coins that have special dates or other characteristics you're seeking.

Make sure you visit your local coin or hobby shop, which sells collectible coins and paper, reference works, advice, coin magazines, storage supplies, and information about local clubs or coin conventions. Clubs and conventions are great places to find dealers and supplies and to meet people who share your interest.

NUMISMATIC BIBLIOGRAPHY

General References

Clain-Stefanelli, Elvira E., and Vladimir Clain-Stefanelli. *The Beauty and Lore of Coins, Currency, and Medals*. Croton-on-Hudson, NY: Riverwood Publishers Ltd., 1974.

Cooper, Denis R. *The Art and Craft of Coinmaking: A History of Minting Technology*. London: Spink & Son, 1988.

Ancient Coins—Greek, Roman, and other European, Middle Eastern, and Indian Coins

Mitchiner, Michael. *Oriental Coins and Their Values. Vol. I, The Ancient and Classical World 600 BC–AD 600*. London: Hawkins Publications, 1978.

An excellent reference for the coins of India, Bactria (Afghanistan and Central Asia), and the various empires and nomadic tribes that occupied these areas over the time period covered.

Sayles, Wayne. *Ancient Coin Collecting*. Vols. 1–6. Iola, WI: Krause Publications, 1996–2001.

An excellent general introduction to the entire field of ancient coins. Volume 1 is particularly useful for its guides to the Web and bibliography.

Sear, David R. *Greek Coins and Their Values*. Vols. 1 and 2. London: BA Seaby Publications, Ltd., 1998.

First place to start for identifying Greek coins from the beginnings in the seventh century BC to the foundation of the Roman Empire by Augustus.

____. *Greek Imperial Coins and Their Values*. London: BA Seaby Publications, Ltd., 1982.

Excellent reference for the autonomous coins struck by Greek cities under the Roman Empire and for contemporary Greek-influenced coinages outside of the Empire. Covers the period from 31 BC to the end of the Roman Empire.

____. *Roman Coins and Their Values*. Vols. 1 and 2. London: Spink & Son, 2000 and 2002.

A good handbook to start with to learn more about the 500-year history of Roman Imperial coinage.

Medieval Coins—Non-Chinese Coinage from Roughly 500 AD on

Album, Stephen. *A Checklist of Popular Islamic Coins*. 2nd ed. Santa Rosa, CA: Stephen Album, 2000.

Broome, Michael. *A Handbook of Islamic Coins*. London: BA Seaby Publications, Ltd., 1985.

Grierson, Philip. *Byzantine Coins*. New York: Methuen Inc., 1982.

____. *Coins of Medieval Europe*. London: BA Seaby Publications, Ltd., 1991.

An excellent survey and introduction to medieval European coins from the fall of the Roman Empire to the start of the sixteenth century.

Mitchiner, Michael. *Oriental Coins and Their Values. Vol. 2, The World Of Islam*. London: Hawkins Publications, 1977.

Monumental work covering all of the coinages of Islamic countries and empires up to the twentieth century.

____. *Oriental Coins and Their Values. Vol. 3, Non-Islamic States and Western Colonies*. London: Hawkins Publications, 1979.

Essentially covers South Asia from Afghanistan through India to Nepal.

Plant, Robert. *Arabic Coins and How to Read Them*. London: Spink & Son, 1973.

Sear, David R. *Byzantine Coins and Their Values*. London: BA Seaby Publications, Ltd., 1987.

Spufford, P. *Money and its Uses in Medieval Europe*. Cambridge: Cambridge University Press, 1988.

Oriental Coins—Coins of the Far East, including China, Korea, Japan, and Southeast Asia

Coole, A.B. *An Encyclopedia of Chinese Coins*. Kansas: Intercollegiate Press, Inc., 1967.

Schjoth, Fredrik. *Chinese Currency*. 2nd ed. Iola, WI: Krause Publications, Inc., 1965.

Easiest to use and most accessible of the English sources for Chinese coinage. Covers China from the beginnings of coinage to the end of the Empire.

Yang, Lien-sheng. *Money and Credit in China: A Short History*. Cambridge, MA: Harvard University Press, 1952.

Modern Coins—World Coinage from 1500 on

Davenport, John S., and Tyge Sondergaard. *Large Size Silver Coins of the World, with Evaluations*, Iola, WI: Krause Publications, Inc., 1991.

Friedberg, Robert. *Gold Coins of the World Complete From AD to 1958: An Illustrated Standard Catalogue With Valuations*. 5th rev. ed. New York: Coin & Currency Institute, 1980.

Krause, Chester L., and Clifford Mishler. *Standard Catalog of World Coins, 1601–1700*. Iola, WI: Krause Publications, Inc., 1999.

Krause, Chester L. *Standard Catalog of World Coins, 1701–1800*. Iola, WI: Krause Publications 1997.

___. *Standard Catalog of World Coins, 1801–1900*. Iola, WI: Krause Publications, 2001.

___. *Standard Catalog of World Coins, 1901–Present*. Iola, WI: Krause Publications, 2002.

Tokens

Rulau, Russell. *Standard Catalog of United States Tokens, 1700–1900*. Iola, WI: Krause Publications, 1999.

Paper Money

Freidberg, Arthur L., and Ira S. Freidberg. *Paper Money of the United States*. Clifton, NJ: Coin & Currency Institute, 2004.

Hessler, Gene. *Comprehensive Catalog of U.S. Paper Money: All United States Federal Currency Since 1812*. Port Clinton, OH: BNR Press, 1997.

___. *The International Engraver's Line*. Cincinnati, OH: Gene Hessler, 2005.

Hewitt, Virginia, ed. *The Banker's Art: Studies in Paper Money*. London: British Museum Publications, 1995.

Kranister, W. *The Moneymakers International*. Cambridge, UK: Black Bear Press, 1989.

Monestier, Martin. *The Art of Paper Currency*. London: Quartet Books, 1983.

Newman, Eric P. *The Early Paper Money of America*. 4th ed., Iola, WI: Krause Publications, 1998.

Pick, Albert. *Standard Catalog of World Paper Money. Vol. 1, Specialized Issues*. Iola, WI: Krause Publications, 1998.

___. *Standard Catalog of World Paper Money. Vol. 2, General Issues, 1368–1960*. Iola, WI: Krause Publications, 2000.

Schafer, Neil. *Standard Catalog of World Paper Money. Vol. 3, General Issues, 1961–Present*. Iola, WI: Krause Publications, 2002.

Medals

Betts, Charles Wyllys. *American Colonial History Illustrated by Contemporary Medals*. New York: Benchmark Publishing Company, 1894. Reprinted by Quarterman Publications. Boston: Quarterman Publications, 1972.

Julian, R.W. *Medals of the United States Mint: The First Century, 1792–1892*. Crawford, IN: Token and Medal Society, 1977.

U.S. Coins

Breen, Walter. *Complete Encyclopedia of United States and Colonial Coins*. New York: FCI Press/Doubleday, 1988.

Newman, E.P., and R.D. Doty, eds. *Studies on Money In Early America*. New York: American Numismatic Society, 1976.

Yeoman, R.S. *Guide Book of United States Coins*. Edited by Kenneth Bressct. Atlanta, GA: Whitman Publishing, LLC, 2006.